INTEGRITY

OF

Faith

INTEGRITY

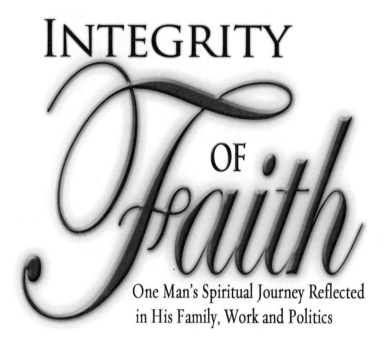

OF
Faith

One Man's Spiritual Journey Reflected
in His Family, Work and Politics

Foreword By Bishop Arthur M. Brazier

Eric M. Wallace

integrity books™

A subsidiary of Wallace Multimedia Group, LLC
www.integritybooks.net

Integrity Books may be purchased for educational, business, or sales promotional use. For information please write: Special Promotions Department, Integrity Books, P.O Box 2281 Matteson, IL 60443.

Dr. Wallace translated from the Greek New Testament all scriptures quoted here.

First Edition

Design by Michelle D. Muhammad of MDM Design

Library of Congress Cataloging-in Publication Data is available on request

ISBN: 978-0-9797631-3-7
ISBN-10: 0-9797631-3-4

DEDICATION

This book is dedicated to my parents, Drs. John and Joan Wallace, whose emotional and financial support through the difficult times of my life was indispensable. To my brothers Mark and Victor for their continued support. Yet, I owe my most profound debt of gratitude, however, to my children, Eric and Greg. This work is especially dedicated to them and the sacrifices they have made over the years.

TABLE OF CONTENTS

FOREWORD

I ntegrity of Faith is a moving biography that attests to the perseverance of the saints in our quest to be faithful to the leading of the Lord. Despite various setbacks, Dr. Eric Wallace presses forward to be faithful in his responsibilities as a father, a minister of the Gospel, a member of an ethnic community, and a public servant with principle—all defined and subordinated by his commitment to Jesus Christ.

My prayer is that as you read Integrity of Faith, you find inspiration to persevere through the challenges and difficulties that cross your path. In the book of Revelation, the apostle John wrote, "And they overcame him [the accuser] by the blood of the Lamb, and by the word of their testimony; and they loved not their lives unto the death" (Revelation 12:11). It is the testimony of sincere believers like Dr. Wallace that attests to the authenticity and veracity of the Gospel, which gives us strength to persevere in our walk with Christ.

Bishop Arthur M. Brazier
Pastor, Apostolic Church of God

"I serve because of my relationship with my Savior. I am a Christian first, a father second, a minister and scholar third, and a black man fourth, and then a Republican. Heaven help me if I ever get these out of order."

PREFACE

I penned these words in a resignation letter to the chairman of the National Black Republican Association (NBRA) in 2005. I had joined a group of black republican activist who saw a need for a national organization. This organization would reach out to the black community, which had predominately voted the Democrat ticket, but in our opinion had seen very little fruit from its blind loyalty to the Democrat Party. In all actuality the black community had seen a great decline in family values and social decorum. This turn of events, many of us felt, began after president LBJ started his "great society" programs, which enslaved the black lower class and shackled them to the US federal government. The result was that a once free and proud people became wards of the state and pawns in the political debate. To the point that the term "black" is almost synonymous with "poor" even though less than 25% of black people are poor.

The words above were written because I believed our black people were being ill served by Democrats and self-serving Republicans alike. I wanted no part of it. My faith informs every area of my life, even my politics. Therefore, doing the right thing, regardless of public opinion, will always be my modus operandi. Faith and integrity must always lead and guide our leaders in the public and private sector, in the pulpit and in the classroom, in the boardroom and on the battlefield. Corruption and disenchantment rule the day when we have lost our faith and integrity. This is evident when our priorities are out of order. My prayer is that I never lose sight of my faith commitment to my Lord, my family, ministry, community and political affiliation, though the latter is more tenuous than the former.

The 2006 US census (p.11) states, "Poverty rates in 2006 were statistically unchanged for non-Hispanic Whites (8.2percent), Blacks (24.3percent), and Asians (10.3 percent) from 2005. The poverty rate decreased for Hispanics (20.6 percent in 2006, down from 21.8 percent in 2005)." The majority of people under the poverty level are non-Hispanic Whites who make up 43.9% of that population.

CHAPTER I

The Christian

A t the formidable age of 16, I gave my life to Christ. I confessed my sins and asked Jesus Christ to be the Lord of my life, to lead me and guide me, to protect and comfort me, to correct me and teach me. He would be the most influential force in my life from here on.

Prior to this, I had been searching for answers to many questions: Who was Jesus? Was he God? Or was he something else? I had been to church but never understood the gospel message. I'm not even sure it was ever communicated to me in the terms that I now understand it. I don't remember the preacher or Sunday school teacher asking any of us if we wanted to receive Jesus Christ as our Lord and Savior.

My parents sent us to Sunday school and church ever since I can remember. Yet I never remembered making a commitment to

Christ. Because of this there was an emptiness that left a void in my soul. Purposelessness blurred my vision of the future and held me captive to fear and aimlessness. But God had a plan for me and I was soon to encounter one of his messengers.

In the summer of my junior year in high school, at a program for minority students interested in engineering, I met Walter Bell at Howard University. He was God's messenger who would share his faith in God and demonstrate it as well. Somehow Walter's life was different. I saw in him strength that I wanted. He shared with me his faith and gave me a tract that explained the "new birth." I must have read it at least five times and prayed, asking Jesus into my life. It wasn't until I had a bad dream that I felt that my confession of faith had taken root.

In my dream I was at a football game but I was not watching the event. My eyes were fixed on a figure dressed in a red suit with horns on the top of his head and a pitchfork in his hand. Yea you guessed right, it was the classical description of Satan himself. He was not looking at me. His attention was drawn toward the bleachers. Then, suddenly a cold chill came over me as the image of Satan in my nightmare started to turn his gaze in my direction. I soon awoke in a cold sweat only to find myself breathing the air underneath my bed covers trembling with fear. After calling on the name of the Lord and peering out from under the suffocating heat of my covers a calming peace came over me. I felt for the first time that God would protect me from the Evil One and that my salvation was sure.

In the eyes of many religious people I did not need a savior. I was a good kid. I never got into trouble. Born on the South side of Chicago on November 17th 1958 to Joan and John Wallace. I was the second of three boys born to the happy couple. We lived on Union Street in a small three bedroom home. I only have a few memories of living on Union.

The first memory, which comes to mind, is how my older brother, Mark, and I set fire to a dollhouse in the backyard. I remember we placed army men in the house at various locations then set it ablaze. I don't remember why we did this or where we got the dollhouse, since we had no sisters. All I remember is watching the plastic soldiers melt as the house went up in flames in the backyard. My brother stood with the water hose ready in case things got out of hand. I guess this is an instance of boys being boys. We never set fire to anything else, probably because our parents weren't too happy with what we did. I don't remember the punishment, but I'm sure there was one. My brother probably got the worst of it since he was the oldest. He was about eight years old, and I was about five. Our youngest brother, Victor, was only two years old.

The other memory I have of Union Street was that of being chased by the neighbor's German shepherd. My brother Mark was riding a tricycle while I was walking backwards trying to get away from him. The next thing I knew he had turned around and started back the other way. I turned around to see the neighbor's dog headed straight for me. I panicked and made the mistake of trying to run from it. I instinctively knew that I could not out run the huge beast so I ran toward another neighbor's parked van. I figured I'd get the van between us and I'd have a better chance to survive. Fortunately for me our neighbor was out in his yard and saw my attempt to elude the beast as I ran behind his van. He came out into his front yard and scared the dog off before it got to me.

To this day I have a healthy respect for big dogs and still wonder what happened to my brother. I guess he was as scared as I was and I am sure he'd say he was going to get help. He had the bike so his getaway was faster than mine. It reminds me of the story of the friends hiking in the woods. One asks the other, what happens if we come across a bear. The other friend says, "run." "But we can't out run a bear," says the one friend. The other friend says, "I don't need to out run the bear, I just need to out run you!" This was my first encounter with strategic positioning, never put yourself in a place where you are the most vulnerable to loss.

With the passing of my mother's parents, William and Esther Scott, we moved to 7201 S. Prairie St. My grandfather was the famous artist, William Edouard Scott. He was a graduate of the Art Institute of Chicago in 1906 and former student of Henry O. Tanner while he was in France. He was married to Esther Fulks. I remember visiting their home on Prairie Ave because   Grandpa Scott used to give us silver dollars. For a young boy of about six years old, in the early sixties, a dollar was a lot of money. I also remember it because he was confined to a wheel chair. He had had his legs amputated because of complications with diabetes.

It was here in this block that I encountered the unseemly side of life. I had received a new bike, a three-speed with flames on the seat. It was a great bike for a seven-year old boy. Unfortunately, other kids thought the same thing. One day when my brother Mark and I were about to go riding a group of kids came riding by and decided to relieve me of my nice bike. Because I was not particularly a good bike rider at the time they cornered us before we could make our get-a-way. We were out numbered two to one, so they took my bike. I don't remember if they got my brother's bike or not. All I remember is getting off and running home. We were basically only a few steps from our house. Next thing I remember is our father driving us around looking for the kids who took my bike. As I recall it we found them and retrieved the bike but it was only a matter of time before it was stolen again. This time we were nowhere around. They took it from the back of the house. Needless to say with these incidences and gang activity not far from the house, my parents packed us up and moved to Wilmette IL.

The town of Wilmette was an interesting place to live for a black couple with three young children. We found ourselves to be the only black family on the block, in the neighborhood, and in the village itself. We left the City of Chicago and a neighborhood where we blended in to live in a Village where we stood out like a grizzly bear on a snow covered plain.

We moved to Wilmette while I was in third grade. I attended Logan elementary school, which was only a few blocks from our home at 806 Park Ave. I remember a story that my mother shared with me about a third grader who found a dime on the playground and turned it in to the teacher. The teacher informed the student's parents regarding what happened, amazed at their son's honesty. My mother tells that story with such great pride, because I was that third grader. I had been taught that if it wasn't mine, it didn't belong to me. It would therefore be wrong for me to keep what was not mine. At an early age, although I did not know God, His principles were being instilled in my life. To this day I give back money if someone has over paid or given me too much change. If I feel someone may miss an item in my shopping cart I make sure they are aware that the items are there. I believe strongly that you do unto others, as you would have them do unto you.

We spent six years in Wilmette. For most of that time when I was in school I was the only African American in class. For most of that time I was the only African American kid beside my brothers in the whole village. Because of this our father, on Sunday morning, would take us to Sunday school at St. Paul AME Church in Glencoe IL. It was his belief that going to a black church would help us maintain our black identity. We would not forget that we were different from the white people we lived amongst.

St. Paul AME church was the first place that I can remember hearing about God, Jesus, and the Apostles, etc. Not that my parents hadn't talked about these things, I am sure they did. My father is an ordained AME minister and started a church when I was just an infant.

The congregation he helped build later became part of the Trinity United Church of Christ. His parents were evangelists. They helped establish a church in Aurora. My dad remembers that on Sundays they were in church from sun up to sun down.

My mother, the daughter of an Artist and a social worker, once considered becoming a Nun. Thank God for my brothers and me she passed up the convent, married our father, had three children and became the first African American to serve as the Assistant Secretary of Agriculture in the Carter administration. Both my parents have some form of religious training so they must have said something to my brothers and me, but I have no recollection of it.

As I mentioned earlier, St. Paul AME church was the first place that I can recall hearing biblical stories. It was probably there where I encountered the biblical heroes of faith that I first began to formulate questions about my own faith. St. Paul AME church would not be the place where my questions were answered. The answers to my now developing queries would have to come later. My father's desire to see his sons retain their black identity seemed to work. At St Paul I met a number of kids I would eventually see again in High school.

Although I had no problem making friends in Elementary school or Junior High, I still knew that I was different. At St. Paul I was just one among many, the people there were like me. They were black. Yet, I was living in a multi-cultural world, disproportionately so. My school was predominately white. My church was all black.

But within each group were other sub groups. In the predominately white elementary school and Junior high I had friends who were Jewish, some German and Italian. They were at various socioeconomic levels as well. I remember attending the Bat Mitzvah for Susan Crown, the daughter of billionaire Lester Crown.

This environment was a great training ground for me. I learned to feel comfortable in any setting whether they be all white settings or all black settings. I learned respect for other people and their different heritages, languages and religious backgrounds. I have never been the fan of "America the melting pot." I have always seen "America as the salad bowl." In the melting pot we lose our distinctiveness and cultural flavor. In a salad the various colors, flavors and textures are added and appreciated for what they bring to the salad. In like manner, the various cultures, racial diversity and experiences make life in the great USA a richer, fuller experience. We can appreciate the differences as well as build bridges of mutual identity without alienating or reducing our various distinctions.

While living in Wilmette I attended Logan elementary, Howard Junior High and New Trier East. I also had my first foray into athletics. I remember coming home from what we called "field day." The schools had track and field competitions and gave out ribbons for first second and third place. There were individual events as well and relay races. I remember coming home from field day at Logan Elementary with a chest full of ribbons. I had placed in the long jump, the fifty-yard dash, the relay race and one more event that I can't remember. I was sure I was headed for the Olympics one day. Imagine my dismay when at the Junior High's field day events I didn't win or place in any of the events (not that I can remember). Although I competed, I did not win. This would not discourage me. When I got to New Trier East, I tried out for the track team. Most of my friends from St. Paul were on the team so I tried out myself. I was a middle distance runner. I ran the 440 and 880-yard dash. My defeats at the fifty-yard dash gave me an indication that I was not a sprinter so middle distance was my ticket. The most memorable part of my track carrier, spanning elementary through my freshman year in high school, was coming in second at an indoor track meet on our home turf. Our school finished first, second, and third.

Track and field was fun and a good learning experience. We rooted for our comrades and they rooted for us. I got to taste victory and defeat. I learned that one defeat does not your life make. Life is full of many defeats and victories. Thus I learned to persevere. I hated practice but knew that to do well in the meets I had to endure the preparation. The pain and toil of the practice made me ready for the main event. So whether I won or lost I was competitive. Winning, I learned, wasn't everything and losing wasn't devastating. Although losing was neither desired nor fun, it did helped me keep things in proper prospective.

In 1973 our family moved from Wilmette, IL to Reston, Virginia. My parents had obtained jobs at Howard University in Washington DC. Thus we moved to a suburb of Washington, this time a racially mixed suburb.

I attended Herndon High School beginning my sophomore year. My first year at Herndon was a difficult year. I was the new kid, awkward, dorky and naive. I was also experiencing my growth spurt. You remember kids whose pants were all of a sudden too short because they had out grown them. They got the nick name "high water." That became my name for a short period of time, until we rectified the wardrobe. I had a few skirmishes, nothing major. I felt I was being tested to see what I was made of. I had begun to take karate classes at school. This was during the time that the T.V. series Kung Fu was popular. One or two more "tests" to see if I knew any karate moves and the testing soon ended. I had stood my ground and earned some respect. A deeper sense of respect would come later after my encounter with Jesus.

This brings us back to the beginning of my story. In the summer of 1975 just after my junior year in High school. I, like most juniors, was trying to figure out what I was going to do for a living. You know, what do you want to be when you grow up? Well the "grow up" part was coming at me faster than I was ready for it. I had no clue as to what I wanted to be. My mother, knowing my propensity to take electrical things apart and put them together, enrolled me into a special summer program at Howard University. It was a two weeks residential program to encourage black youth to consider engineering as a profession and of course attend Howard University. I was a sixteen year old about to stay on a college campus and be away from home for the first time in my life. I looked forward to some newfound freedom.

The program started in late June or mid July. I was supposed to share a room at the end of the hall with another student who never showed up. I had the room all to myself. My room shared a bathroom with another adjoining room. In the adjoining room was Walter whose father was a preacher and whose life was defined by his faith in Christ. During the program Walter would share his faith with me and invite me to his parents home. I was impressed by their love for each other and for their faith in God. What impressed me the most was Walter's dedication. One night the program gave a dance for the members of the program and the residences of Meridian Hall. I was at the party for a while then realized Walter wasn't there. I went up to his room to see what he was doing. I walked in on him while he was on his knees praying. I had never seen devotion like that before, especially in someone my age. My soul was stirred. I wanted what he had. He later gave me the gospel literature that I mentioned earlier in this chapter and I gave my life to Christ.

I returned home and to school a bible toting Christian. I went to Church (Walter's home church in Wash, DC) regularly and began reading the bible. I still have my first bible, the Living Bible. It has my signature, address, date of purchase (10/6/75), my age, height and weight listed in the inside cover.

Soon my mother would direct me to a church in Reston, so I would not have to make the trip to DC. The church was led by a Rev. Butler in the multipurpose room of an elementary school. I would receive my call to preach under his ministry. It would be God who would determine what I would be when I grew up.

CHAPTER 2

The Family Man

In June 22, 1979 I married Andrea, an attractive young woman I met and fell in love with while I was working at Sears and attending Howard University (HU). I was only twenty years old. She was nineteen. When we married I was attending Washington Bible College (WBC) studying for the ministry. I received a call to minister the gospel at the tender age of seventeen and left HU's electrical engineering program to study ministry at WBC.

It was love at first sight. I caught glimpse of this beautiful girl who worked in Sears' catalogue department walking through my sales area and had to inquire whom she was. She had long flowing black hair and caramel skin. Her mother, a very attractive woman herself, was from the Cape Verde Islands. Her eyes were big and sparkled when she smiled. She was very shapely as well. She came around enough for me to strike up a conversation. We later started dating and one thing led to another and we were married.

Unfortunately, this world of bliss I was living in would soon come crashing down. In my senior year at WBC I almost dropped out of school. Our marriage had hit a speed bump but I thought things were fine. We were under financial strain like most newlyweds but we were making it work, so I thought. She was working full-time for a credit Union. I was going to school full-time and working part-time.

To my surprise and sheer agony I came home one day from work that evening to find another man in our apartment. They had been drinking champagne on the couch. After he hastily left, I confronted her about what happened. She insisted that nothing was going on. My fears were later confirmed when I found a letter she had written and thrown away. It was clear that tearstains were on the letter addressed to her male "friend." As it turns out he had been a love interest from high school. One in which the two of them never got together, until now. She thought she could see him without getting attached but he dropped her and went back to his old girl friend. I confronted one of her best friends over the phone to tell me what was going on. She finally confirmed that Andrea had been romantically involved with this guy.

I was devastated. It was as if someone had punched me in the stomach and then tried to extract my heart via my esophagus. The pain was excruciating. The timing, as if there ever is a good time to find out your spouse has been cheating, was incredibly bad as far as school was concerned. I had taken more classes so I could graduate that year (1981). I thought the sooner I graduated, the sooner we could focus on life, love and our careers. One night she came home around 4:00am. I was so hurt and upset I made her pack up and move back in with her parents. I was also upset with God. I felt that this should not happen to someone who had devoted his life to ministry, been abstinent until marriage and currently studying for ministry. This was not supposed to happen. Why God! Why me?

We were together for a year and a half. We were married three years. I did graduate as planned. But going to school and church while your life is in turmoil is not easy or fun. I still had to study, write papers and take exams. I was in charge of Children's church at First Baptist Church of Vienna Va. Where Rev. Butler was now pastor. What should have been a year of celebration became a year of mourning. I graduated from Washington Bible College June 16, 1981. I was divorced in 1983. The later event would change my life more than the former.

I had tried to restore my marriage after our separation, but to no avail. I had always believed that once you married you stayed married and worked out your problems. I had been hard on my parents, who had gone through a divorce some years earlier. What I learned is that it takes two people to make a go of it and if one wants to end the marriage they can. She did and I was wounded for the first time in my life.

I now faced the Christian world with a big red "D" on my chest for divorce. Many doors closed to me after my marriage failed.

There are those who would never let me teach, preach or serve in their churches, bible colleges or seminaries. This experience, though it broke my heart, helped me become more compassionate and empathetic to the plight of others. Heartache is no respecter of persons. It also made me more introspective and self-aware.

Even though I was at times angry that God allowed this to happen, I was also aware that without His presence, I would have given up. I would have dropped out of school and no telling where I'd be. I am a firm believer that tragedy and hardship either draw you closer to God or draw you away. The choice is ours to make. I chose to draw near. But this would not be the last time that tragedy would strike my household.

A few years later I got married again. This time the marriage would last seven years and produce two boys, Eric and Gregory. But it would also end in divorce eight years after we had said our vows, "till death do us part."

I married Charis, 7 1/2 years my junior who had just graduated high school. She had a statuesque beauty about her. She was a dancer with magnificent legs. Hindsight and my introspective mind led me to think that our marriage failed for three reasons. It failed, because I had not fully healed from the first divorce. I was lonely and looking for companionship, but had not given myself enough time to mend. Secondly, it failed because although I cared for her, I was not in love with her. Therefore I did not give her the attention and affection a husband should give his wife. Shortly after we married I moved the family to

Mt. Vernon New York so she could be near her grandmother and I could go to seminary. We lived in an apartment above the church where I served as the Youth Minister. I worked part-time for UPS at night and attended Alliance Theological Seminary (ATS) in Nyack NY during the day. Our first born, Eric, was only an infant. Charis stayed home and took care of Eric.

These days were hard. Money was scarce, work was laborious and seminary was challenging. That first year was very stressful. As the Youth minister part of my job was to take the church van on Sunday afternoon and pick up the teens that lived in the Bronx. I would then teach a teen bible study to them and other teens in the neighborhood. After bible study I had to drive them back to the Bronx and return home. When you add participation in Sunday morning service, it turned out to be a long day.

The new week would begin with classes, homework and working at UPS. The strain on the marriage was tremendous. Charis and I fought constantly because, I believe, I did not give her the attention she needed and deserved. I spent most of my time away from home. I was under stress from work, school and ministry. She was under stress from taking care of a newborn by herself, in an apartment with few if any amenities. The church we lived in was located in the heart of Mt. Vernon between the rift raft drug dealers and the business section of town. In the church apartment where we lived she was pretty much isolated from others. I later gave up the UPS job and working at the church and moved the family on campus for my second year of study.

On the seminary campus Charis would have other women to socialize with and I would be closer to school and my professors. To make ends meet I worked as a security guard at night that allowed me to study. Charis sold Tupperware and did quite well.

Although our living conditions improved, our relationship remained volatile. Our arguing reached a height that our neighbors across the hall offered to help us pay for counseling. We attended counseling and I also decided to change my degree program from the three year Master of Divinity to the two year Master of Arts. I thought that finishing school would help bring peace to our family and allow us to focus on the family and earning a living.

Neither of these moves helped. We left seminary with a number of issues unresolved and a big debt owed to the school. I had finished the course requirements but needed to write a paper or take an exam to fulfill the degree requirements for the MA. But I first had to pay off a mounting tuition bill.

We left Nyack NY for Lake of the Woods in Orange Co. Virginia. We were in debt, tired and now had two children. Our second son, Greg, was born in Suffern NY May 31 1988. We settled in a house located on the lake owned by mother and stepfather. My mother had married Maurice Dawkins, a minister who had worked for OIC as a lobbyist, and was now running as a Republican for US Senate seat against Chuck Robb. My mother, although she was an independent, must have liked Republicans. My natural father, who had been an administrator at Howard University, was also a Republican. I would later drive for Mr. Dawkins in his campaign, which would be my first taste of the political scene, but not my last.

Upon settling in we figured it was time for Charis to use her skills and fulfill her dream to own and run a dance studio. There were plenty of new shopping centers around and we found one that was interested in permitting a dance studio in their center. We scraped the money together to pay for the hardwood floors and even did some of the work ourselves. I remember staying up half the night working with Rev Butler who said he knew how to lay a vinyl floor. These were large continuous strips of vinyl used to cover a dance floor that was not going to have hardwood. This was the smaller of two rooms. The larger one had the raised hardwood. The smaller room had raised vinyl. We spent a lot more time on that floor than either of us had expected. By the time we had finished we were both exhausted with glue all over the place. It took a few days to eventually get all the excess glue off the dance floor. Charis' dance studio was open for business!

Unfortunately our marriage seemed to be closing down. Soon we left the Lake of the Woods to be closer to the dance studio. I joined the Fredericksburg police department, but things still were not right at home. We seemed to grow further apart. She was involved with the studio and I was trying to pretend like I wanted to be a police officer. I thought I could marry ministry and police work, but that never happened. The dance studio, which was supposed to be our main "bread and butter," began to have financial problems. We moved the studio to a new location and then tried to modernize to keep track of revenue and expenditures. We bought a computer and computer software to help manage dance studios.

Eventually I quit my job with the police department and came to work at the studio. I believed that we needed to streamline our operation. I would be the janitor, accountant, graphic artist and whatever else needed to be done. I saw this as a way of saving money and making the studio work for us. Charis saw it as my meddling in her business. Shortly after this move we found ourselves living in different households. Charis moved out and found another place. I stayed in the house, kept the computer, and started my own company, Wallace Publishing and Computer Graphics.

Our children, now 5 and 3, were in private school. Eric was in first grade and Greg was in pre-school. Since I was working from home I watched them Monday after school until I dropped them off for school on Friday. Charis had them from Friday after school until Monday when she dropped them off at school. This arrangement worked because their mother had to work from about 2:00 pm to 10:00 pm.

It was hard to see my family torn apart. I would have done anything to spare our sons the tragedy of a broken family. But it was too late. I had missed opportunities to try to mend the relationship, but was never sure my heart was ever fully there. Hindsight, they say, is 20/20. I believe I married too soon after my first divorce. Loneliness, companionship and sexual desire are prime motivators for many who remarry before they are completely healed, especially for Christians who believe that sex outside of marriage is inconsistent with biblical principle. But what I failed to realize is that a broken heart unhealed is a heart incapable of love. It is like a sponge that can't absorb or a tongue that can't distinguish flavor. An unhealthy heart can't reciprocate love. Like a broken mirror it will only distort its reflection.

If blame were to be assigned, I would place it at my feet. I was older, had been married before, and I was the head of my household. I feel that I failed in my leadership responsibilities in the home. The sense of failure divorce brings is sometimes overwhelming, especially to committed Christians. This is not supposed to happen.

Knowing that divorce is a social ill that many times gets passed on to the children of divorce, I was even more motivated to become the best father to my sons. I was determined to model behavior that they could emulate as they matured into men. My prayer was that they would never have to taste the pain that I had suffered, twice.

As mentioned earlier the boys stayed with me most of the week. While they were in school I worked my business, Wallace Publishing and Computer Graphics. When they got home I spent time with them, cooked dinner and cleaned up after I put them to bed. I was now a single father for all practical purposes.

Charis and I separated in 1991. We were divorced in 1992 or 93. All I remember is getting the final papers just before my birthday and thinking what a birthday present. Although these days were difficult the most excruciating part of my life would come in just a few years. The business venture I had embarked upon began to run out of operating capital. After three years it was clear that I could not afford to keep the house we were living in. My father had helped us purchase the home and was helping me make the mortgage payments in this emotionally and financially difficult time. We had to sell the house. It also meant that I would be moving back to Chicago more than 800 miles away from my sons.

In a few short months I lost my house, my business and, most of all, my ability to see my boys whenever I wanted. My time with Eric and Greg would now be relegated to summers and every other Christmas. This would be the arrangement for the next six years. When I left Virginia my sons were seven and five.

The move to Chicago was filled with anguish. I was returning to my place of birth a battered and bruised man. I had left everything I loved behind. But there was an assurance that this was not the last chapter in the life of Eric M. Wallace. God was not finished with me yet. I knew that some day my sons and I would be reunited on a more permanent basis. The only other bright spot, beside my faith in God, was attending the Apostolic Church of God (ACOG) with my younger brother Victor and his wife.

I had attended ACOG in previous visits to Chicago. I knew that Bishop Brazier was someone I could listen to every Sunday and possibly find a way to get involved in ministry there. I knew that one day I'd sit on the rostrum with the other ministers. For I was a licensed minister with a BA and not quite finished MA in biblical studies, there must be something I could do in this Church, I thought.

But things would get worst before they got better. I moved to Chicago with a promise of having my own apartment. My father owned a thirteen-unit apartment building and had promised to keep one available for me. By the time I got to Chicago he had rented out the apartment and I had to stay with him. This was not what I had in mind! Two grown men living in a one-bedroom apartment even though they were father and son did not make for peace or privacy, especially since I had been living in a three-bedroom house. On top of this, add the fact that there were not many jobs available. I ended up taking a job with the Board of Education packing school supplies for shipment to various schools. On days where they had too many packers, since I was the one with the least seniority, I was sent to the docks to sweep the floors. I believe this was the lowest time in my life to this point. I felt like Joseph in Pharaoh's dungeon. With all that had befallen me I was now being stripped of any self worth or pride. Not that I believed that I was better than those around me, but I felt that my education and skills were not being utilized. I did not go to college and seminary to sweep floors at the department of education. But if I had to sweep the floors, I'd be the best floor sweeper they had. And I was.

These were trying times for me. I missed my sons. I mourned the loss of my home and business. Working at a job that did not appreciate my abilities was humbling. Later being laid off from that job was even more humiliating. I needed the money. I had to take care of my children with child support. I was wounded, humiliated and exhausted. If I had not been a Christian at that time it is no telling what I would have done. But despite the circumstances, in my spirit, I knew things would get better. God would take care of me like he took care of Joseph, Daniel and Jeremiah. All of these biblical characters felt abandoned at some point in their life. I began to believe that the hardships we face in life prepare us for the great task God has for us to perform. He strips us of everything to empower us to be his vessel. Remembering the saints of the Old Testament confirmed that I was in good company. Moses had been in exile for forty years before he returned to Egypt to be God's agent of deliverance. Galatians 6:9 says "Let us not be discouraged in doing good, for at the appointed time we will reap a harvest if we don't lose heart" (my translation). There is a distinct time in which God flips the script and those who have struggled to do good will see their efforts come to fruition if they do not lose heart, give up or lose their resolve. Perseverance is the key. Through my hardships I learned to persevere. The true characteristic of any leader, worth following, is perseverance. Then add to that character and integrity. I was learning that persevering in the classroom was not enough. Perseverance in life is what makes a man. Anyone can quit when things get rough only those with strength of character remain standing through the trials of life.

I would eventually get my own apartment and work around the apartment building doing odd jobs for my father. I'd repaint an apartment, fix a hole in the wall, cut the grass, shovel the snow etc. It was still not very glamorous or fulfilling but I was blessed to have a father who supported me with a roof over my head and food to eat.

When my sons visited for the summer, we'd be cramped in the one bedroom apartment but we had fun. They were able to visit with their grandpa and uncles. We visited all the museums in Chicago, at least once over the years. Navy Pier, miniature golf, video arcades, and movies were constant places of entertainment. As they grew older I was able to take them to a Cubs game, a Bulls game and a pre-season Bear's game. I felt that a father should take his sons to at least one sporting event. I wish I could have done more. Money was scarce during those years, but you learned to make it stretch for memorable occasions.

The most difficult part of having them for the summer or Christmas was that the time flew by so fast. Within a few short weeks I was getting them ready to fly back to their mother. Saying goodbye always brought tears to my eyes. I never allowed them to see me cry. I did not want my tears to be the last thing they saw before they got on the plane. I would wait until the plane pulled away from the gate and in the early days watch the plane take off. Fighting back the tears, I'd take the lonely walk back to my car. I'd then take the lonely drive back to the apartment, praying their safe return home. Once at the apartment, I'd enter the now quiet and lonely apartment and reflect on the fun we had in anticipation hours later of a phone call that said they had arrived safely.

This scenario would continue for six years. I'd see them twice a year for basically ten weeks out of fifty-two. Two weeks at Christmas and eight weeks during summer break were all I had of their growing and learning experience. To this day I feel like I'd missed a large significant part of their growing up. In that six-year period I had them for less than sixty weeks. (I did not get them every Christmas.) But I knew that one day the situation would be reversed. I was a firm believer that sons need their father. And in another sense fathers need their sons. It is difficult to fulfill your role as a father from hundreds of miles away. But I did what I could. I was determined to stay in contact with my sons so I called at least once a week.

In the summer of 1999 my prayers were answered and for the first time in six years my sons and I would live under the same roof. I had moved to Virginia to study for my PhD. After finishing the coarse work (1997-1999) their mother asked if I was ready to take them. After a millisecond of hesitation I told her, "yes, of course." At the ages of thirteen and eleven, Eric and Greg moved back to Virginia to live with their dad.

We would only be in Virginia for a year but that was a memorable year. I was studying for comprehensive exams. My program required us to take five, four hour, exams in two weeks. You studied and read, read and studied until you thought you were ready then you took the exams. During this preparation time my boys were in eighth grade and sixth grade. I sent them to a private Lutheran school just a few blocks from the seminary campus. The school had a special rate or scholarship for seminary students otherwise I wouldn't have been able to afford it.

My routine in the morning was to get them up and fix their lunches while they ate breakfast cereal. Once they were off to school

I'd get dressed and head over to the seminary library. There I would study until the boys returned home around 3:15 pm. I'd fix dinner while they did their homework and watched TV. It was during this time that they introduced me to their favorite program, Dragon Ball Z. When they were younger I'd watch cartoons with them. Their favorite cartoon was Winnie the Pooh. I grew up on Pooh, Tigger, Piglet and Eeyore and so did they. Now they were introducing me to their favorite martial arts anime. I was hooked. We watched it every day, Monday through Thursday, on Fridays they'd show something else.

This routine only changed when soccer season started. They both were on the Luther Memorial soccer team and I went to every game. I was the proud dad running up and down the sidelines making a spectacle of myself. But I didn't care. I was proud of my sons and of the team. They made it to the championship game. Although they lost, it was a memorable season. One my boys have not forgotten. It was the first time that I got to see and partake of a sporting event that my sons had been involved in. They had played soccer and tried out for football but I was not around. They were with their mother. So this was special for me. This was heaven on earth. As I look back on it now I am so glad I was a part of this experience. It was the last time both Eric and Greg would play organized sports together. It was the only time that I would be able cheer for both my sons at a sporting event.

During this incredible year I was also the interim pastor for a Presbyterian Church. So as a part of my routine I'd start writing my sermons on Saturday morning before the boys got up and finish it after breakfast. Once I had finished the initial draft I'd take them to the park or a movie or just go walking through the mall. Saturday afternoon we tried to do something fun. Sunday morning the boys got to hear their father preach the gospel.

This was an exciting and incredible year. Having my sons back, watching them play sports, pastoring a church, and passing my comprehensive exams. All these things made my life rich once again. But nothing could compare with being a fulltime dad again. I had missed being a father and now I was enjoying it all over again. To top all this off Eric graduated from eight-grade. 1999-2000 rates as one of the best years (school year) of my life.

After passing the doctoral exams I decided to move back to Chicago. The church where I was an interim now had a pastor. There were no jobs in Richmond Va. that I could see. So we packed up and moved to Chicago where I would again work for Urban Ministries, this time as their director of editorial. I would buy a house in Matteson IL. My boys would attend school at Rich Central high school and Huth middle school.

Since moving to Matteson the past seven years have been very eventful. I have watched my sons grow into young men. Eric graduated from Rich Central high school in 2004. He was on the track and field team for three years. He was a member of the French club and a past President. As of the writing of this book, Eric attends Columbia College. Greg graduated from Huth Jr. High in 2002 and then from Rich Central in 2006. Greg was a mathlete for three years.

He was also a member of the French club and past vice-president. Greg was a member of the French honor society. As of the writing of this book Greg is matriculating at the University of Illinois Chicago Campus as an Illinois scholar.

Both sons graduated with better than a 3.0 and it was the first time they had the privilege to stay in one school district for more than two years. Up until this point they had moved from one school district to another. When we moved to Matteson I was determined to give them stability in their schooling. That meant no moving out of the district until they'd graduated.

Over the years God has blessed me with the opportunity to travel with my sons all across the USA. From Washington DC, Florida, and Las Vegas, we have driven almost clear cross-country. My hope and prayer is that the time we spent together helps them continue to grow into the men God would want them to be, despite the short comings of their father. Every father's prayer is that their sons become better men than they were, men of great faith and uncompromising integrity.

The failure of my marriages will always haunt me. I wish I could have modeled for my sons what it meant to be a good husband. But someone once told me that if I modeled the traits of a good man it would translate into being a good husband. For me that means giving one's self wholly to the service of God, without reservation.

If anyone desires to come after me, let him deny (disregard) himself and let him pick up his cross daily and follow me. For whoever desires to save his life shall lose it, but whoever loses his life for my sake shall save it. Luke 9:23-24

CHAPTER 3

The Minister and Scholar

The call to ministry came when I was seventeen years old. I had become involved at a new church in Reston VA. The pastor, Rev Butler, held services in an elementary school. I used to come early and help him set up by putting hymnals on the chairs. I guess he saw my dedication to Lord and one day asked me to preach. I knew nothing about preparing a sermon. Nor did I have a clue as to what to say. I remember my parents being in the audience and I remember sharing my testimony. I declared that everyone must be born again quoting John 3:16. The most significant thing I remember about this first sermon, if you can call it that, was the fact that people started crying. I joke that my sermon was either really bad or the spirit of God was touching peoples hearts. I still have not determined which it was.

By the time I was twenty-two I was licensed to preach, Rev. Butler was pastoring a Baptist church and I was matriculating at Washington Bible College (WBC) in Lanham Maryland. Rev. Butler and I had become good friends. About twenty years my senior he was like my big brother in ministry. He had encouraged me to study for the ministry and gave me opportunity to teach children's church and later to become the Youth Minister.

One of the most significant turning points in my life came while I was watching the 700 Club hosted by Pat Robertson and Ben Kinslow. My early days as a Christian fed off of the 700 club programming. Ben Kinslow and his persona on TV inspired me. It was clear that he loved the lord and had a good grasp of the gospel message. Besides that he looked like me, he was black. I was a regular viewer because of Ben.

One day they aired a special program with Bill Bright, president and founder of the Campus Crusade for Christ ministries. Bill was talking to a group of college students about my age. I don't remember his message though I am sure it had something to do with commitment to sharing the gospel. All I remember is his invitation at the end. I was moved so much that I believe it was this event that changed my life and my ministry for Jesus Christ. After his talk he called upon everyone in the audience to make a commitment. He said if you are willing to serve God and go wherever He wants to send you, even if it means you may be in danger of losing your life, I want you to stand to your feet. I was sitting in the basement of my mother's townhouse in Arlington Virginia. I stood to my feet. It was at that moment that

I believe sealed my determination to serve Christ wherever he sent me. It solidified my commitment. It strengthened my resolve and bolstered my faith. Come hell or high water I was in for the long haul. Little did I know that this new found resolve would be tested time and time again.

Subsequently, I left Howard University to study for the ministry at WBC. My parents were not too happy with this idea because I was receiving a tuition break at Howard. They both worked there. But I felt the call to ministry and a need to be prepared. Howard had no undergraduate religion courses so I felt I had no choice but to leave.

While studying at WBC I was challenged to think about getting an advanced degree. One of my professors wanted me to think about attending their seminary and then return to WBC to teach. At the time they had no black professors but a growing number of black students. I was flattered by the interest but I knew that this was not the course for me. WBC had some doctrinal stances that I was not in full agreement with and to teach there you had to be able to sign a statement that you agreed with all of their doctrine. I believed that all of the sign gifts were still operating in the church. They did not.

The three years at WBC taught me a great deal. My first encounter with biblical languages was there. I learned to read Greek and Hebrew developing a taste for exploring the bible on a different level. I was exposed to sharing my faith in a systematic way. Every semester they have a week where teams of students would go out in an organized fashion and share the gospel. Some would go to the airport, some to malls, others would go into the inner city and do open air evangelism. Open-air evangelism generally targeted children but also provided opportunities to talk to adults as well. They would drive to a spot where there was a nice size crowd of people nearby. They'd set up a canvass to do a "chalk talk." Although they generally used paint on the canvas the presentations were developed for use on a chalkboard. The team would garner interest by telling the kids and adults that we were going to be doing a presentation. We would use gospel magic and sing songs to get the crowd interested. Then someone would get up before the canvass and begin to share the gospel message while drawing or painting words or figures as they related to the story. At the end, we would ask if anyone wanted to receive Christ as his or her savior. Then we would pray with them and for them. Anyone who prayed with us was given a card to fill out so we could direct him or her to a church and follow up on his or her progress.

I took this basic concept and used it in the church. I was in charge of children's church at First Baptist Church in Vienna Va. Children's church consisted of children ages five to ten years old. We would sing and play games. I might use a gospel magic trick then I'd share a chalk talk with the kids and then pray with them. I did this while I was attending WBC. I can't remember a specific figure but we had a number of children accept Christ as their savior over the years I spent leading children's church.

I also became responsible for the youth ministry at First Baptist. By youth ministry I mean teenagers. I organized the ministry establishing the mission, purpose and goals. I organized an adult advisory group that would help with events and supervision. I established a weekly bible study and a monthly schedule of events. We went camping, to amusement parks, skiing, and picnics. The most rewarding part for me was seeing teenagers begin to understand that God had a purpose for their life. Then to see them begin to trust Him and walk in faith.

Most of these things happened while I was at WBC. My intention upon graduating was to become a fulltime Youth minister. What no one told me was that there weren't many black churches with fulltime Pastors, let alone youth ministers. I was beginning to see the difference, for the first time, between the black church and the white church. Many white churches had paid staff; assistant pastors, youth pastors, children's pastor etc. Black churches had a pastor. I was not to find gainful employment as a youth minister. It was also during this time that my first marriage fell apart limiting my options for ministry opportunities.

In June of 1981 I graduated from WBC knowing that I wanted to learn more also knowing that job opportunities were scarce. For a short while I started a ministry called Y.M.I. It stood for Youth Ministries Inc. The purpose was to help churches, especially black churches, organize a youth ministry. It was a non-profit Para-church organization that depended on the donations of others to keep it functioning. Needless to say raising money was a difficult task and YMI only engaged one church. I would soon give up on YMI and in a few more years I would let go of the idea of fulltime Youth ministry. I learned through this experience that perseverance is sticking with something until you've gotten all you can get from it or give to it. Then you move on to something else and try to make a difference there. Far to often in the name of persevering we continue to ride a dead horse and wonder why we are not progressing. Its time to find a new horse!

My new horse would have to wait. I joined the Army National Guard. They sent me to boot camp at Fort Benning Georgia. I immediately became a squad leader and toward the end of boot camp became the platoon leader. I was there to learn Fire Direction Control for the 81 mm mortars. They were the ones who received the coordinates from the forward observer. They would then calculate the settings for the mortars to hit their target and give those settings to the gunners.

When I returned to my unit I found out that there was a position for a chaplain's assistant. I applied and was accepted for that position. After going to military training for chaplain assistants I began to drive the chaplains around during our weekend drills and two week training in the summer. The funny thing about this position was that I did as much ministry work as the chaplain. Most of the chaplains had churches and would not stay for the Sunday half of weekend drills. So I would perform their duties. I'd teach or have a short service. I'd pray with soldiers and sometimes even counseled them. I liked it so much I decided I wanted to be a chaplain. But to become a chaplain you had to be ordained and have a master's of Divinity (MDiv) degree. I had neither of these credentials. I was licensed but not ordained. These requirements were part of the impetus for my seeking graduate level studies. I would later begin the process by enrolling in seminary at Virginia Union School of Theology and filling out all the paper work for becoming a Chaplain candidate.

As a Chaplain candidate I had the rank of Second Lieutenant and was considered a Staff Specialist for the United States Army Reserve. Before I could become a full fledge chaplain I would have to finish the MDiv degree, be ordained by a recognized denomination and finish Chaplain training. I would never finish the process. My wife was afraid that I'd be called out to war if we ever had one and she'd be left to take care of our sons. Because of her concerns I gave up my commission. I served in the Guard for about eight years from 1982 to 1990. I was a chaplain assistant for most of that time and a chaplain candidate for about two years. I enjoyed the ministry in the armed forces. I enjoyed wearing the uniform, the camaraderie and being proud to serve my country. If I could do it again I would. But she was right I would have been called up for desert storm and the Afghanistan/Iraqi war. But that wouldn't have been something that I would shrink from. I understand the sense of pride and honor of the men and women who wear the uniform. Many of them serve with great distinction and with great pride put their life on the line for their country. I prayed with these men. I counseled these men. Hiked up hills and walked through the bush with these men. I would have been proud to go to Kabul, Baghdad or Tehran with these men. I still wonder today where I would be if I had stayed in the Guard.

Although I left the guard I still had a hunger for more biblical knowledge. I moved our family to New York so that I could attend Alliance Theological Seminary (ATS). I started out in the MDiv program for Urban Ministry. I later changed my degree program for the following reason. First, I did not need the MDiv for the military since I was giving up my commission. Second, I was now looking at a PhD and did not necessarily need an MDiv for doctoral work. Lastly, it would shave off a year of study and my wife and I were having problems at the time. Completing the master's program sooner sounded better than later.

The ideal for further graduate work was solidified at ATS. My emphasis in the Master of Arts program was switched to Old Testament. I was fascinated with the Hebrew language and, at the time, my Hebrew bible comprehension was greater than my New Testament Greek. I was also amazed at the reading ability of one of my Hebrew professors, Dr. Widbin. He read Hebrew as fast as he read English. We had a hard time keeping up with him when he would read the Hebrew text in class. I wanted to be able to do that. I was also a big fan of the Old Testament (OT) stories of overcoming obstacles through faith. I firmly believed that the Old Testament was key to understanding the New Testament. I still believe that to this day. Although my OT professor inspired my desire for doctoral work it was a New Testament (NT) professor, Dr. Crockett, who spoke directly about further study. He had spoken to me about a paper I had written for his class. I was one of the only two who received an "A" on the exegetical paper we were assigned. He called me into his office and talked with me about continuing toward the PhD. At the time my interests were in Hebrew bible, not the New Testament. The amazing thing is my attitude would change years later and my conversation with Dr. Crockett would take on a prophetic air.

My time at ATS was full of good times and hardships. As mentioned earlier my wife and I were struggling to keep our marriage together. Yet at the same time we enjoyed watching our first born, Eric, begin to develop his verbal, motor and social skills. Our youngest son Greg was to be born while we were in New York also. My final venture at Youth Ministry occurred while in New York. As I mention in Chapter two, I worked as a youth minister at a church in Mt. Vernon. I was responsible for the programming and bible teaching for the teens. This was something I enjoyed but found that I could not pay the bills doing this. Ultimately after a year of full-time seminary, working at UPS, Youth Ministry, a new father and husband, something had to give and it was I. I was exhausted, but learned a great deal. I loved everything I was doing but there wasn't enough of me to go around. I needed to be ministered to. I was running on empty, looking for a gas station and none could be found.

I learned to never place ministry, school or anything before family. God does come first, but that is personal relationship not ministry. My personal relationship with God must come before everything else. If I do this then the rest of my relationships will begin to fall in order. Many ministers feel that their ministry is of utmost importance and that is wrong. Our families are our greatest ministries. This was a hard learned lesson.

We left ATS in June of 1988 with our newborn son Greg (one month old), our almost two-year-old son Eric, and no MA degree. I still owed the school money and thus was not allowed to take the final exam or write a paper. Hence I did not graduate. It would be eight years before I would come back to claim the Master of Arts in Biblical studies degree with an emphasis in Old Testament.

In the meantime, my family moved to back to Virginia to a town right outside of Fredericksburg. There I would start my own publishing company, Wallace Publishing and Computer Graphics. I really had no computer graphics training. I learned what little I knew by watching others. Before my wife and I separated I was helping with the dance studio and watched a graphics person put together a program for the dance recital. It didn't look that hard. So after we went our separate ways I began to develop an idea for a Christian yellow page directory. The Washington DC area had one called the *Shepherd's Guide*. I called mine the *Lamb's Book*. We did two editions of that directory, which double its size in one year. But I wanted to do something more substantive than a directory. So I started a magazine called the *New Life Journal*. Its purpose was to showcase people in various walks of life and have them share their testimony. I believe that a shared testimony is the best witness for the gospel a person can hear. It gives hope to the Christian and challenges the non-believer to believe.

I had a number of people help me with this endeavor. We had no money to pay anyone, so we bartered for photography and stories. It was my first foray into publishing and although there were not funds to continue, it would not be my last. I liked publishing a magazine; it was a lot of fun. It was also a lot of work and cost a lot of money. Hence we only did three editions and had to fold our operation. This episode in my life ignited the desire to incorporate my biblical knowledge with publishing.

After the business went under, I moved back to Chicago. After a number of odd jobs (see chapter 2) and a few years went by, I had and opportunity to return to Virginia to do some work for my mother who needed some publishing done. I laid out a newsletter called *Towards Democracy*. It was while I was working for my mother and her organization, Americans for Democracy in Africa, that God worked a blessing out of a misfortune.

Before I traveled back to Virginia in 1995 I had been playing the conga drums for the Angelic Choir at the Apostolic Church of God (ACOG). They had a big concert coming up so I made plans to fly back to Chicago from Baltimore's BWI airport. When I returned to BWI my car, a late model Mercedes Benz, would not start. I had bought this car a number of years before and had planed to restore it to its original luster. It was a rare 280 Coupe. But it would not start. I was in no mood for car trouble. I was so tired from the trip, besides it was cold and raining outside. I could not imagine that God would turn this lemon into lemonade. I called my former pastor knowing that he had a friend in Maryland, another pastor. I got his number. Called him and he came and picked me up. We had the car towed to a Mercedes dealer and had it checked out. I spent the night at his house. During my brief stay at his home I had a chance to share with him my plight. I shared how I had wanted to sell the car to pay off my school debt at ATS. I told him how frustrating it was to have finished the work for a masters degree without having the degree in hand. God must have spoken to his heart because he offered to buy the car from me at blue book value subtracting the cost to get it fixed. I accepted the deal. It gave me a little more than $3200.00. This may not seem like much but it was exactly half the money I needed to pay off my school bill. But that's not all. While I was in Chicago I had a conversation with my father about this outstanding school bill. He had promised that if I could come up with half of the money, he'd pay the other half. God is Good! When I had the check in hand for the Mercedes, I called my father and said I have my half!

In few short months I had paid off my bill. I flew out to New York to ATS to take an oral exam. In May of 1996 I was walking across the stage receiving my Master's degree ten years after I had started it. I had the chance to just get it in the mail but I thought that I had worked too hard and waited too long to not walk. I also wanted my sons to see their father receive his degree. I felt a great weight was lifted off of my shoulders. I had wanted to apply for entrance into a PhD program but could not because I had not finished the masters. I was now free to pursue doctoral work.

A few months later I was accepted into the Master's program at Union Theological Seminary in Richmond Virginia. I had applied to the doctoral program but the committee suggested that I try the

Masters of Theology (ThM) program first. I was disappointed to say the least, but not down cast. I was told that if I did well in the ThM program I could transfer into the PhD. Both programs covered the same material. The ThM students were in the same seminars as the PhD students. Basically, the ThM students did the first year of the doctoral program then received their degree. If they were accepted into the PhD program before they graduate they would just move into the doctoral program and not receive the ThM.

I was ready to accept the challenge. I had been out of school for eight years so I was a little rusty. Besides, I knew this was my destiny. It had been delayed for some reason beyond my comprehension, but now the doors that had once been closed, were now wide open and I was running through them.

I spent a larger part of my life moving between Illinois and Virginia. Each time I came back to Va. I'd move a little further south. This time it would be Richmond, the capital of the confederacy but I was not intimidated. I would be attending one of the top tier seminaries in the country, Union Theological Seminary. Its sister school was Princeton Theological Seminary in New Jersey. Union only accepted four students every year into its Biblical studies program, two for New Testament and two for Old Testament. Their faculty was well known throughout the Biblical field. Achtemeier, Kingsbury, and Carroll were names well known in New Testament studies. Mays, Towner, McBride, and Brown were names well known in the field of Old Testament studies. Union was a good school and very selective.

There were four Masters of Theology (ThM) students and three PhD students. I was one of the four. We were all in the same seminars, writing papers, giving presentations and defending our points of view. We studied both Old and New Testaments. Our degrees were in biblical studies. The demarcation in focus between Old and New Testaments came when we began our comprehensive exams and our dissertations. It was very intense, but I was having fun. Two of the ThM students went on to study for the PhD. The other two went into pastoral ministry. I was one of the ThM students but my entrance into the program would be delayed.

My acceptance into the PhD program would make me the first African American to enter their biblical studies program. But as I stated this would be delayed, and as some once told me, "delayed does not mean denied." God had a plan to which again I was not privy too. I applied to the PhD program in Old Testament while matriculating in the ThM program. I was active on campus in the black student group made up of MDiv students. They were all sure I would get in. I would be the first. My grades were good. I was not as confident. I thought I would get in, but did not think it was a shoe-in. Unfortunately I was correct. The committee turned me down. I couldn't believe it. I called the head of the graduate studies committee to find out why I was not accepted and I got a list of reasons to which I gave solid answers in reply. I did not hear one solid reason for why I was not accepted into the program. I was there doing the work like the rest of the PhD students. My grades were good (2A's and a B). I was told that I needed an MDiv degree, but the other person they let in did not have an MDiv either. After my phone debate with the Graduate Studies Committee Chairman, I spoke with the head of the Biblical studies department, Dr. Carroll. He told me that the New Testament department had two positions open because the people they had invited to study at Union chose other schools. He was open to taking me on. I was open to switching to New Testament.

I then spoke with the president of the seminary, Dr. Weeks, to see what could be done. He said that he did not have the authority to override the committee, but he could ask them to take another look at my application. I agreed. They took another look and determined that they should not change their ruling and set a precedent, but that I should reapply next year to be reconsidered. I was disappointed in their decision, but I did all I could do.

Somewhat discourage and unable to find work in Richmond, I returned to Chicago with a ThM in biblical studies. Again, I did not know that God had a plan especially designed for Eric M Wallace. When I returned to Chicago I found work with the only African American owned Christian education publishing company. They published Sunday school, Vacation Bible School and other church related Christian Education materials. I came on as the assistant to the director of editorial. I worked under the director of editorial, Rev Alice Dise. I was only at Urban Ministries, Inc. for about five months when I received a letter saying I had been accepted into the Biblical studies PhD program at Union Theological Seminary.

Once again I moved back to Richmond Virginia, but I didn't mind because I knew this was part of my destiny. I would spend two years in Richmond before I would return to UMI as the director of editorial. Those two years were full of hard work and great reward. I learned a great deal and was challenged to think outside the box. I matured to the point that I could now appreciate the differences in theological debate. I finally realized that I did not have to agree with someone in order to learn from them. Sometimes disagreement can be helpful and informative whether you change your position or not. As the old saying goes, "iron sharpens iron." The mental gymnastics and the intellectual weightlifting began to hone my perspicacity. I was seeing things from a different perspective. Challenging my preconceived notions and those of my classmates and professors was enjoyable, and a lot of work.

I also began to see why my entrance into UTS was delayed. First I was to make contact and work for Urban Ministries. Second, two of the adjunct professors I had were only there for the year I returned and that was the last year that I took classes. The following year I prepared for exams. Professor David Hay from Coe College stands out as one of the visiting professors that I am glad I studied under. He was instrumental in helping me formulate my dissertation project. Another professor who came to work for UTS while I was in Chicago was Frances Taylor Gench. Dr Gench would become the chair of my dissertation committee. She would see me through the ups and downs of writing and rewriting a dissertation. She would also steer me through the dissertation defense.

I am not sure how it would have worked out if I had been at UTS when I wanted to be there. I am not sure how things would have worked out if I had not met Dr. Hay and Dr. Gench when I did. Taking nothing away from the other professors at UTS they all helped shape me in one form or another and I am grateful for their scholarship and their patience in dealing with me.

In June of 2000, after passing my comprehensive exams, I would once again pack up and move to Chicago to go to work for Urban Ministries, Inc (UMI). The Lord had directed my steps back to publishing and I was eager to take on the new position. I was returning to Chicago "ABD," which means all but dissertation. All I had left to do was write a 200-page book demonstrating my ability to incorporate all the scholarly tools I had been honing in class. Completion of the dissertation and a successful defense gave me the admission card into the scholar's club. I could call myself and be called by others a "biblical scholar" with doctor attached to my name. I would become the second Dr. Wallace, my mother being the first in our family. I looked forward to that day. I also remembered that it would be an historical milestone. I would be the first African American with a PhD in Biblical studies from UTS. I never forgot that sense of responsibility. It kept me going at times when I thought about giving up. The fact that others were counting on me to complete what I had started would be a great motivating factor for me. My friends and members of the black caucus at UTS, my sons, my parents and those who would follow in my footsteps gave me the impetus to finish the long arduous journey.

The journey to completing the PhD would take a detour. Working fulltime at UMI was not conducive to writing a dissertation. There was no time to do research and one can't write a dissertation without research. Beside that I had a full plate outside of UMI. I was also working as a consultant for Bishop Brazier and the Apostolic Church of God. I was helping them revamp their training program for ministers. It was a great experience. I worked with some good people. We worked hard, but I enjoyed it. Add to this the fact that I was a single father who came home every night to cook dinner and make sure homework was completed, you may understand how not one word of a dissertation was written. But I was somewhat content. I enjoyed what I was doing and I was getting paid for it. I was making more money than I had ever made. My life was full. Except for a spouse, I had everything I wanted. I had a house, two cars, two jobs, two healthy boys, a condo in Ft Lauderdale and a timeshare in Orlando.

But there was that dissertation that needed to be completed. What was I to do about that? I did not have the time to devote to researching, writing, editing and rewriting with everything I was doing. So something had to give. The Lord must have agreed with me because a year after being hired as the director of editorial I was laid off. I had been there a year and a month. The company was going through some financial difficulty and needed to lay off a few people. I was one of them.

At first it was difficult to see how God would get glory out of this. Yet, as I thought more about it, and I had plenty of time to think, I realized it was a golden opportunity to finally tackle that dissertation.

UMI gave me a nice package, continuing my health benefits for a number of months and income for a month or two. It was not great but it helped soften the blow. I then had to make some decisions. I was either going to find a new job or work fulltime as a student again to finish the degree. I chose the latter. But it came at a price. I sold my condo in Florida, my second car and eventually my timeshare. The money was not flowing like it used to. I took out student loans to supplement the lost income but it wasn't enough to live at my former income level. I still had the church income and that helped me make ends meet. So until graduation I was a full time student, a fulltime single parent, a Christian education consultant.

It was a challenge, but again, I felt this was part of God's plan. There was no time to lose heart, get upset or waste time. God had given me an opportunity to finish the dissertation and I had planned to do just that. His grace and favor was extended to me when I was given an opportunity to use the library shared by the Lutheran School of Theology at Chicago (LSTC) and McCormick Theological Seminary (MTS). Because both McCormick and Union are Presbyterian Schools, McCormick extended me the privilege of using their library and allowing me to have a study carrel. These carrels were given to those doing advance theological work. They were small rooms with a desk and a light. It had a lock on the door so you could leave materials in the carrel without fear of someone taking them. We were allowed to check books out of the library or to our carrel. Without these privileges I would not have finished the dissertation in the timely manner that I did. I was also given access to the University of Chicago Library. I was certified as a visiting scholar with all the rights and privileges.

The Lord had opened the door. It was up to me to do my part. He had provided what I could not provide for myself. He had made a way where there had been no way. He gave me access to that which was closed to me before. In His timing He made the impossible possible. I would get the boys off to school then leave for school myself. I would be back in time to cook dinner and make sure homework was done. I met with the church committee one day a week either before or after I had been to the library. The dissertation was my job. The church was my part time job. Fathering my boys was a lifetime responsibility. I enjoyed them all.

I was laid off in February of 2002. Two years and three months later I would graduate with my PhD in biblical studies. It took me seven years to complete the program, five if you subtract the time spent at Urban Ministries. In that time, five years of actual study, I came away with two degrees, a ThM in Old Testament and a PhD in New Testament. Now tell me that God isn't good! Perseverance was the key. Perseverance was enabled by faith. Believing that God had called me to do what I was doing. Faith believes that even though you cannot see the path before you, you know the destination. I knew the final outcome. I would finish.

Therefore, May of 2004 holds special significance for my family and me. We had two graduations and a birthday to celebrate. My eldest son Eric graduated from High school a week before I graduated. My son Greg celebrated his 16th birthday a few days after I graduated. It was an amazing month. I had the chance, along with their mother and sister who flew in from California, my mother and father who flew in from Florida, to watch Eric walk across the stage. My sons and my parents all went to Richmond Virginia to watch me walk across the stage. Then we went to Williamsburg Virginia to celebrate Greg's birthday. These were all significant events in the Wallace household, ones we will never forget.

Soon I was teaching biblical studies as an adjunct professor for Elmhurst College and North Park University. I was also still an associate minister and working as a consultant at the church; teaching the Pentateuch and the Gospels. However, my greatest honor as a minister was to remarry my parents who had divorced in March 1978. They had both married again, but became single. My father went through another divorce and my mother became a widow. They soon began to date each other and one thing led to another. On October 25th, 2003, after 25 years apart, I remarried my parents in the home of my younger brother Victor. My elder brother Mark gave our mother away and Victor served as the best man. I was the preacher. It was an amazing event.

But a political event would take place and change my outlook on ministry and politics. It was the presidential election of 2004. My life would soon change as God began to direct my footsteps down another path.

Family

L to R: My Parents, Victor, Eric (me), Mark

Artist: William Edouard Scott painting Mrs Scott

My eighth grade graduation

Family

Dr Joan Wallace (Mom), Dr. Eric Wallace, John Wallace (Dad)

Me and my brothers: Mark, Eric, Victor

Parents Wedding

Military

Eric, Dad (me), Greg

Greg, Dad (me), Eric

Public Servant

Veteran's Day parade

Veteran's Day parade participants

Martin Luther King III

State Senate Fundraiser

Fundraiser

Graham Fundraiser

Candidate Forum

Dr. Wallace, Newt Gingrich, Dad

Bishop Simon Gordon

GOP Chairman Ken Mehlman

*The ultimate measure of a man is not where he stands
in moments of comfort and convenience, but where he
stands at times of challenge and controversy.*
—Martin Luther King Jr., *Strength to Love*, 1963

CHAPTER 4

The Black Man

Growing up in a predominately white environment and being born in the late fifties I was aware that I was different. I remember stories that my father told me about his childhood. How he was called the "N" word as white boys chased him home from school. He had to run to keep from being beat up. His was a hard life of poverty and racism. By the time I came along things had gotten better but not their best. I remember hearing about Martin Luther King and the march on Washington. I was just five when it happened and ten years old when MLK was assassinated. I remember being called the "N" word but don't remember any of the particulars. I just remember an unpleasant feeling and wanting to punch someone in the nose or turn and run, neither of them were things a young boy or grown man should have to endure.

On the positive side I remember being proud to know that my mother was appointed the first African American to serve as the Assistant Secretary of Agriculture during the Carter administration. She worked for four presidents and became my standard of accomplishment. I remember pulling for black athletes in the Olympics and when they won feeling so proud, especially if they were the first in their particular event. They encouraged me to do better. When the Washington Redskins won the super bowl with Doug Williams as their quarterback I was ecstatic. Not just because I was a Redskin fan, but Doug was the first African American quarterback to win the Super bowl. It was also a personal victory because sometime before a white associate told me that a black man could not be a quarterback. He said blacks where better at running and leaping and not leading a team or throwing down field. Clearly he had never heard of Warren Moon.

Therefore, I am elated whenever stereotypes about blacks are broken. I rejoice when the psychological impediments of blacks and whites are laid to rest in the graveyard of ignorance. I am a firm believer that there is nothing that a white person can do that a black person can't do. The question only revolves around being willing to pay the price. For many blacks the price has been very high, but they persevered anyway and achieved great things. Sojourner Truth, Frederick Douglas, Hank Aaron, Paul Robeson, overcame many obstacles to do what they did. Blacks have made contributions in every area of study and practice, in the Arts, Sciences, and Humanities. We have excelled in sports, music and other forms of entertainment. Despite the obstacles, despite any hardship and despite many odds against us we succeed.

But this is true of anyone who applies themselves to a task regardless of their race or ethnicity. This is why I appreciate the salad bowl metaphor rather than the melting pot. The salad bowl does not require or suggest that we lose our ethnic or racial distinctiveness but it values those differences that bring flavor and texture to the salad. Translate this to real people and the salad bowl metaphor appreciates the uniqueness and diversity. It does not strive for homogeneity.

This allows me to be proud of my black heritage and legacy without offending my white brothers and sisters. It allows whites to be proud of their heritage without being anti anything. I am proud of my African heritage. I am also proud of my Native American heritage. I am also proud of my European heritage and claim William Wallace as one of my ancestors, whether he is or not!

To be a black man in America means to always remember that others are watching you. Others are sizing you up to see if you measure up, black and white. It means that if you are the first to do anything you blaze a trail for those to follow. It means there is a little more pressure to do the right thing, make the right decision and be a man among men. It means trying to live down the stereotypes that the media continues to perpetuate. It means taking a stand when others take a seat. It means providing for your family, not only the bread to eat, but a safe haven for your kids and your spouse. Even if she makes more money than you, you are to provide the atmosphere for her and your kids to thrive. You are the launching pad for their greatest. You are the pit stop for their passion, the oasis for their journey. You enable, empower, encourage, council, counsel, and console. You are the man!

Many of these lessons I learned the hard way from the mistakes I made along the way. As I raised my sons I believe I became more of a man. Understanding that their lives were in my hands and that we only get one chance to do it right made each moment one of a lifetime.

I was blessed to be able to make every soccer game my sons played. My father made it to only one of my track meets. His job did not afford him the time to make other meets. I was blessed to be able to take my sons on a number of vacations where we drove across country to go to Florida, Virginia, and Nevada. We also went on two cruises to the Bahamas. As a child our family took a number of road trips. We enjoyed them immensely. I was blessed to give this experience to my sons.

The challenge of being a man is not allowing yourself to be defined by your occupation or the amount of money you make. The legacy of the African American people extends through the tragedy of slavery. Black men and women were treated like animals, with no rights, privileges or respect. But they persevered despite the maltreatment and humiliation of being owned by another human being. If they had allowed themselves to be defined by their occupation and the malicious treatment they endured, they would have never bought their own freedom, or escaped to freedom. And once emancipated they had the audacity to become doctors, lawyers and served in congress. It is this legacy that helps fuel the fire that burns in me. If slaves and former slaves could endure the hardship they faced and still make something of themselves, how dare I not endure the few inconveniences that I encounter along my journey.

The journey to manhood meant working jobs that were not to my liking. I do not wish to denigrate any form of "gainful employment," but many of the jobs I have worked down through the years were not pleasant experiences. Although I have learned a lot about myself, some experiences I'd rather not repeat. I have already mentioned working for the board of education and sweeping floors. Another job like it was working at the CIA building in Langley VA.

I was taking classes at Virginia Union School of Theology in Richmond. (Not to be confused with Union Theological Seminary also in Richmond.) I was taking classes on the weekend and working fulltime at the CIA building stripping and waxing the floors. I was working the night shift Monday through Thursday but on Friday's I'd work the day shift. Then Friday afternoon I'd drive from Arlington Virginia to Richmond to take a Friday night class and a Saturday morning class.

There was a team of us who'd strip the wax off of a large section of floor then lay a new coat of wax on the same floor we had just stripped. We became very good at what we were doing. The problem was you never knew who was going to return the next night. People were fired left and right because they could not pass the background check. It was not my ideal job but it helped pay the bills.

It is amazing how many people pass you by without noticing you exist, when you work a low skill level job. I was determined that once I ascended to wherever I was going to ascend too, that I would not treat people the way some people ignored or looked down on me at the time. I was contributing to society. I was newly married and trying to make something of myself.

One pleasant incident that took place while at the CIA building was a conversation that lasted only a few minutes. A young woman engaged me in conversation and said that she had heard that I was a spiritual leader. I was struck by that characterization of me. I had never though of myself as a spiritual leader, but I was. I was a licensed minister of the gospel and had been for a number of years. I was studying to earn a Master's of Divinity so I could become a chaplain in the National Guard. Yet up to that moment I had never seen myself as a spiritual leader. I had let my current paid position redefine who I was. Even though I was working toward a lofty goal I was still viewing myself from where I was, not where I was going.

Now there is nothing wrong with a job as a custodian. If you feel that custodian work is your calling then do it and do it well. Ultimately, if custodial work is your passion own the business don't settle for being an employee. Become the head of the department. Stripping and waxing floors was not my passion. It was a means to an end. I used it to meet my needs while I went to school. But I had begun to allow the work I was doing to define who I was. They are not one and the same.

The Bible tells us that God made humans in His image. Although there is a debate among scholars as to the exact meaning, it is clear that God gave Adam dominion over God's creation (see Genesis 1:26-28). Humans are given authority to rule the planet, in this we are somehow like God. We carry some kind of divine seal that we belong to God. Gen 9:6 warns that capital punishment is reserved for those who murder other humans because they (humans) are made in God's image. This idea is affirmed in the gospels when Jesus addresses the question of paying taxes (see Mark 12:13-17; Matthew 22:15-22; Luke 20:20-26). In an attempt to trap Jesus, he is questioned about whether people should pay taxes. Jesus asks for a coin and asks his opponents whose image is on the coin. The answer is Caesar's. Jesus then replies render to Caesar that which is Caesar's and to God that which is God's. The parallel inference is that we are like the coin but the image stamped on us is the image of God. Therefore we should render ourselves back to God because His image is on us and thus we belong to Him. Showing due reverence to God is to give oneself back to the Creator.

Understanding that we belong to God and somehow carry His image means we ought to see ourselves in a different light. Unfortunately we allow ourselves to see each other through distorted spectacles not the eyes of our Creator. God sees people worth dying for (John 3:16). We see a people we wish would die. God sees people worth spilling His own blood. We see people worth exploiting. God extends his grace. We extend credit and indebtedness. God sets people free. We enslave and make people captive. This is the world that we have created and the one that God seeks to deliver us from. Deliverance is a process that starts with the spiritual, being born again then leading to the physical, emotional and psychological.

My encounter with the woman at the CIA helped me see myself in a different light. I experienced a readjustment of how I thought.

I would not allow others to define who I was by what I was doing. Nor would I define myself, or others by human standards. I am a man made in the image of God called into His service to help liberate others from the shackles of humanistic thinking. It is my calling to encourage people to render to God what is God's. This call would later find expression on a political platform. But for now I would learn more and more about myself and my strengths and weaknesses as I moved from job to job and continued my education, in and out of the classroom.

Another memorable job that I had, which I believe helped shape me was that of a police officer. My stint as a cop was only about thirteen months. I joined the force believing I could marry ministry and police work. I could "protect and serve" and minister the gospel at the same time. I knew others who had done it; maybe this was what I was supposed to do.

It soon became apparent that there were some on the force who did not like the fact that I was a minister or black. The town of Fredericksburg was looking to hire new police officers, especially minorities. Their force was predominately white but the city had a growing black population. They were seeking diversity in their department, so I applied.

While at the academy I ran into trouble with the shooting range instructors. I was an average shot. Although I had been through military boot camp and fired an M16 I had never fired a handgun. I was not a very good shooter. I believe the instructor planed to use this as a reason to get rid of me. One day we were shooting at the range and one of my fellow trainees told me that he would shoot more rounds once we got closer to the target than when we were further away. This was cheating. You were supposed to shoot off ten rounds at 100 feet, ten at fifty feet and ten at twenty feet away from the target. (These are not exact distances. I do not remember what the exact distances were. This is just to give you an idea). We would start further out then move closer to the target. Knowing that I was not the best shooter in the group they figured I'd take the advice of my fellow trainee and cheat by saving a shot or two until I was closer to the target. What they did not know was that trying to concentrate on the target and count the rounds I shot was more than a notion for me. I would lose count and have to ask the instructor beside me how many I had shot. I remember one time I had too many bullets left in my magazine. This was not cheating, it was an inability to shoot well and keep track of rounds fired. I could not have cheated, if I wanted too.

I was accused of trying to enhance my score. We went before the commander and I pleaded my case. He must have believed me because I ended up going to another academy outside of Fredericksburg. He could have just fired me on the spot. I drove to Waynesboro, Virginia. to start academy training all over again. But to my dismay I would not finish. I was injured while playing volleyball after hours. Because there wasn't much to do in Waynesboro we found a pick up game of volleyball at another site. I went up to spike the ball and came down on the base of the pole that held the net up. I twisted my ankle so badly I had to wear a cast. I would not be able to finish the academy until the next class came through. Once I had recovered fully from my injury I returned and finished the training. The third time was a charm.

During those intermittent times when I wasn't at the academy I had a chance to ride shotgun in the squad car. I also got to taste the attitudes of my fellow officers—those who liked me, and those who had a bone to pick with me. The police force is a tightly knit group. You are either in or out. Although there were others who were on the periphery of the main group, I was out because I did not act like the typical rookie. I was much older. I was a minister and I was black. As I remember it there were only two other black policeman on the force. They were both veterans. One had come from a neighboring counties sheriff's department.

To this day I cannot tell you for sure whether my failure to bond with some of my colleagues was because I was black, a minister, or refused to conform, or possibly all of the above. I just knew that this was not my cup of tea. One of the final straws was riding with another officer who had an ax to grind with me. It was at night and I remember him pulling over as we argued about something. We even got out of the car as if were we going to fight. I guess I was supposed to back down. That was not my character. Maybe I was a little cocky back then, and maybe he thought I was supposed to "suck up" to him. Whatever the case, we never rode together again. I would later quit the force and work full-time at the dance studio, which my wife was running.

It was not hard to see that police work was not my calling. Some on the force tried to get me fired. Some had tried to force me out. I left in my own time at my own choosing. It was after this that I would eventually begin my own publishing business and be bitten by the entrepreneurial bug. I would fall in love with publishing and marry that with ministry.

Throughout my various working experiences I have always learned something about the job, about the people who work these jobs and myself. I have a great deal of respect for those who serve in what we call blue collar jobs. I have great respect for those I worked with as a police officer. Not all of them where jerks. Actually, there were more good cops than bad. You just remember the bad ones more. Just because it was not my life's work or calling does not detract my respect for those who feel called to serve or work in fields I choose not to.

I have a healthy respect for the police, the military, service workers, and a host of others, because I have walked in their shoes. I have rubbed shoulders with them, fallen down and gotten back up with them. I think these experiences have prepared me to be a better person, minister, father and man. The hardship I have faced in these jobs just made me more determined to press on, to serve God, wherever He places me. I think it places me in a better mindset to see people for who they are and as God intended them to be. I did not come to this understanding until I began to think about running for public office.

Another incident that caused me to reevaluate my job history was when I applied for a position at a well-known Christian publishing company. The gentleman conducting the interview looked at my resume and commented on the number of and types of jobs I had over the years. He then commented that he had been at the same job for over twenty years. The implication was that he was somehow better. I chose to see it that my experience was richer, not better or worse. When one goes through various jobs that seem to have no bearing on your future, one starts to second-guess some of those choices. You even begin to ask God where you made the wrong turn. Because one's life has taken a different path than most, one feels they must have done something wrong. But I believe God has a plan for everyone and that plan does not conform to conventional wisdom most of the time. It is our job to be obedient and follow His leading wherever it takes us.

I would find myself in a place of inquiry, seeking God's direction shortly after finishing my PhD and teaching as an adjunct at North Park University and Elmhurst College. My eyes would be opened to the political arena. I would soon put to test the second half of Dr King's quote that heads this chapter. Here is the full quote:

> The ultimate measure of a man is not where he stands in moments of comfort and convenience, but where he stands at times of challenge and controversy. The true neighbor will risk his position, his prestige and even his life for the welfare of others. In dangerous valleys and hazardous pathways, he will lift some bruised and beaten brother to a higher and more noble life. Dr. MLK Jr. Strength to Love, 1963.

Risking ones position, prestige and life is what a person does when they run for office. If they win they are celebrated. If they lose they are consoled and sometimes forgotten. Whatever the case they spend time, money and effort to have a chance to make a difference in the lives of their neighbors, friends and countrymen. I would take on this challenge and run for State Senate in the 19th district of Illinois in 2006. In a state that was full of corruption and greed it was my belief that you are either part of the problem or part of the solution. I decided to be part of the solution for "to whom much is given much is required" (Luke 12:48).

*I am a Republican, a black, dyed in the wool
Republican, and I never intend to belong to any other
party than the party of freedom and progress.*
—Frederick Douglas

CHAPTER 5

The Republican

I graduated from seminary in June 2004, with a PhD in Biblical Studies. That fall I was teaching at North Park University and Elmhurst College as an adjunct professor. At the same time I was beginning to look around to see what God had in store for me. As a doctoral student most of the world was cut off to me. In order to finish a dissertation one needs to hide in a cave and not come out until you are finished. And even then you don't engage the world until you defend your dissertation. A dissertation defense (for us) was sitting before all the professors in our discipline, other graduate students and even the general public and answering questions from anyone who wanted to ask one. This was the place where you demonstrated your command of the subject material. This experience would come in handy in the next phase of my life.

It is only after the defense that I was free to leave the cave and once again engage the world. Having come out of the cave, I began to take notice of the presidential election. I had started voting Republican since Reagan ran against Mondale. I came to appreciate the moral principle upon which the GOP stood. As a Christian I could not reconcile the seemly anti-Christian stances of many of the left. Add to that the support of Gay rights, abortion on demand, and fear of public displays of religious faith, I could not find a place within the Democrat Party. They represented everything that I felt was wrong with the world.

So I began to watch the GOP convention with much interest. I had always liked President Bush. I felt that he was strong in his principles and sincere in his personal faith. He struck me as a man who took a stand regardless of the political consequences. If he thought he was right he would stand-alone if he had too. I felt that John Kerry had no principles and every decision he made was calculated to gain the maximum number of votes. I watched the GOP convention for more than one day for the first time in my life. When the president of the Untied States of America took the podium, I could see in his eyes the conviction from which he spoke. Those same eyes would well up with tears as he spoke about the sacrifice of our military in the war on terror. I did not see the villain that the papers, pundits, and black preachers railed about. I saw a man of conviction and fortitude, a man of character and compassion. I was inspired to believe that Christians in politics could make a difference. One does not have to be "sleazy" to run for office. One can engage in the public debate and run for office with real convictions.

After the election was over, I read an article in the Chicago Tribune about a group of Baptist pastors and ministers who had met in Nashville, Tennessee. They had discussed how they could effect the election for the Democrats in 2008. This article distressed me. I could not understand how these black preachers could not see what I saw in President Bush and the Republican Party. Most of these men were against Gay rights and marriage. Most of these preachers believed in the sanctity of life. Most of these men and women believed in personal responsibility and rejected dependence on the federal government. Most of these preachers wanted better education for their children and housing for families and opportunity for success. All these things were part, in some form or fashion, of the Republican Party platform. I did not understand the disconnection. I did not understand their disdain for the Party that abolished slavery (13th amendment), made us full citizens (14th amendment) and gave us the right to vote (15th amendment). Did they not know that the first blacks to serve in Congress were all Republican? Did they not know that the Klu Klux Klan was organized by the Democrats to stop blacks from voting Republican? Where they ignorant of how the KKK raped, murdered and burned our people as agents of the Democrat Party? Had they forgotten it was the Democrat Governors, in the 60's, who closed their schools so blacks could not attend? Were they ignorant of the role Republicans, specifically US Senator Everett Dirksen, played in pushing through the Civil

Rights act and the Voting Rights act? Were they aware that Bush had more blacks in his cabinet than Clinton? The list goes on and on of the superior civil rights achievements of the Republicans over the Democrats. Are most of us just ignorant of the facts? I believe the answer is YES!

I soon began to feel that as a minister of the gospel I needed to make my voice heard. If the other preachers were going to proclaim the Democrat Party as the party for us someone needed to challenge that false perception with reality.

I began looking for a black Republican group I could join. My mother and father had been members of a black Republican group in Florida so I looked for the same here in Illinois. I called the Cook County Republicans, the Illinois GOP and the RNC. I was determined to become part of an organization that would help spread the message of the Republican Party. But to my dismay I found remnants of a once vibrant group that seemed to be on its last leg. I also found another group but it included Democrats and Republicans. Its chairman had positioned himself in leadership for life. He was the King with no intention of relinquishing the throne anytime soon. I could come and be a serf in his kingdom. But I was not interested in a political group with no identity. Nor was I interested in joining a group to bolster or expand his kingdom. I was looking for a chance to change the maligned image of the Republican Party in the black community.

Eventually this led to the establishment of the African American Republican Council (AARC) of Illinois. I took the by-laws of one of the Florida groups and adapted them for Illinois. Along the way I ran into other likeminded black Republicans from which we formed an executive board and in 2005 officially became a 527 group. Later that year we were approved by the State Central Committee to use the word "Republican" in our name. We became an affiliate group of the ILGOP

Our goals were listed as follows, as taken from the original set of by-laws: The objectives of the AARC OF ILLINOIS shall be to:

a. Develop a strong, effective and informed AARC OF ILLINOIS: and expand AARC OF ILLINOIS membership.

b. Increase African American Republican registration.

c. Provide a communication bridge between the African American community and Republican leadership of Illinois.

d. Promote an informed electorate through political education.

e. Encourage AARC OF ILLINOIS membership of Republican Party participation and political involvement, at all levels of government.

f. Support the principles, objectives, and platform of the Republican Party and help secure the election of all duly nominated Republican candidates in the General Election and registered Republicans in non-partisan elections.

Our objectives were simple and clear, hence as I edited them I felt a responsibility to take on the idea of being more of an ambassador to the black community. I began to think about running for office. This would, as the proverb says, "kill two birds with one stone." I could take the message about the party directly to the people and build the organization. I could also win a seat and help with the dismantling of the culture of corruption in the state of Illinois.

These were lofty goals. Yet I felt we had to aim high, and I had to lead the charge. Although I was a novice I felt that my credentials as an ordained minister and a PhD would open doors that might otherwise be closed. This idealism and naiveté would soon be shaken with an encounter with reality.

I found a number of people interested in becoming a part of AARC. We began having meetings on a monthly basis. Attendance fluctuated between 15 to 25 people every meeting. Our first year, we experienced tremendous growth and accomplishment. Here is the letter I wrote to the members and those thinking about joining at years end.

To the Members of AARC of Illinois: Our first Year

As I look back over the year I remember the good and the bad, the joys and the sorrows of trying to get an organization off the ground. I must stop and thank God for His favor and guiding my every footstep. I thank Him for bringing men and women into the organization that share the same vision that I share. No organization that aspires to make a difference can accomplish anything with just one person. It takes others willing to work hard and sacrifice to see the vision come to fruition. As a group we have seen AARC transform from an idea to a reality. And as we look to the coming year we anticipate that AARC will be a force in Illinois' politics.

These are only a few of our accomplishments for 2005:

1. We incorporated and became a 527

2. We began holding monthly meetings in April

3. We ratified bylaws

4. We picked interim officers

5. We have a logo

6. We have a temporary meeting place

7. We have around 15 members but are averaging 25 people at our meetings

8. We held our first fundraiser and made money! (over eighty people attended)

9. We have three people running for office.
   a. Glenn Harris for State Representative, 8th district
   b. Marc Wiley for State Representative, 80th district
   c. Eric Wallace for State Senate, 19th district

10. We have become an affiliate organization of the Illinois Republican Party

Thus I am grateful for the hard work of current and former members of the executive board. Former members include, Patrick John, Warren Ballentine and Erick Nickerson. Current board members include, Elroy Leach, Delores Westbrook, Will McNeil, Anthony Anderson, Glenn Harris, and Eric Wallace. We are adding at least two more members to the board, Frank Penn and Richard Irvin. As AARC continues to grow we will also need to grow the executive board.

This next year, 2006, holds great promise for AARC. We have an opportunity to help elect three of our members to the state legislature. There are others thinking about aldermanic positions and positions within the party organization (committeeman). We have a chance to help elect the next Republican Governor of Illinois and other statewide, county local officials. By doing this we will increase Africa American participation in the Republican Party and state government.

As stated above, 2006 will be a great year for growth and opportunity. But we need the help of those of you of African descent, who name the Republican Party as their party of choice, to get involved. We cannot do this alone. We need your gifts, talents and connections in order to be the organization, I believe, God has called us to be. So I call on those of you who have been standing on the sidelines to come help this organization move to the next level. Help us emancipate the African American community from the plantation of the Democrats and transform the thinking of both whites and blacks. There is a lot to do and so few workers. The eyes of the IRP and RNC are now on us. Soon the black community will be scrutinizing us. Let us therefore be sure of our purpose and goals. Let us not veer to the left or to the right but be steadfast in our objective. For we know that ultimately it is the Lord that we serve not we ourselves. So come join us and help us make a difference in 2006.

Have a blessed New Year!

Eric

Rev. Eric M. Wallace, PhD
Chairman, AARC of Illinois

Unfortunately success sometimes breeds contempt. Shortly into 2006 a schism broke out among the board. A few board members felt that I could not lead the group and run for office. They moved to get rid of the vice-chairman (whom I had chosen) and replace him with their preference. With a loophole in the bylaws, all they needed was a simple majority to expel anyone on the board, including the founder and chairman, me. For the first time I was confronted with a mutiny. They had conspired behind my back while I was in Washington DC at a BAMPAC[2] meeting where Lynn Swann, candidate for governor of Pennsylvania was speaking. They would take control of AARC by getting rid of my vice-chair and replacing him with one of their people. Some of the questions and concerns that they had were legitimate, but they went about it the wrong way. Instead of calling a meeting to discuss the issues that concerned them, they took action then wanted to discuss why they did what they did. Dismissing my vice chair, without consulting me, then putting me on notice, did not sit well with me. From that moment on I did not trust the members who partook in that event.

Eventually they would have to go because I wasn't going anywhere. One by one we got rid of the conspirators. One was removed for incompetence. One was about to be removed for incompetence until we noted that his term was up. The vice chair only served for one year. He was to be chosen by the Chairman then confirmed each year. Well his year was up. I was not about to confirm him. The last person quit after all his friends were off the board.

I learned an important lesson from this. It is not enough to have people on your board who agree with you politically. They need to be in agreement with you ideologically and hopefully morally. Disagreement, however, is not a bad thing. It allows for various views to be explored and addressed before a decision is made. The problem comes with those who have hidden agendas. You cannot solve a problem or address an attitude if you don't know it exist. Secondly, your by-laws need to state clearly how you deal with conflict. There were no stated reasons for removing a board member. You did not need to show just cause or allow a person an opportunity to defend themselves. All you needed was for someone to gather a majority of board members then vote you out.

Needless to say, we now have a new set of bylaws. We accomplished very little in 2006. The fighting with board members and running for office took its toll on the organization and on me. I was ready to "throw in the towel." I had been advised to do so by friends and family. But I did not start AARC for myself, but for those like me who wanted to socialize with other black Republicans and who wanted to share their ideas and principles with those outside the party. We see organizations like AARC as a tool to bring about change in the party itself, in the community, and change in the political process—all changes for the better. To let AARC die is to give up on the vision God gave to me. To this day I am not ready to do that.

The thought of running for office was quite a notion in and of itself. My political experience was limited at best. I had driven for a US Senate candidate while living in Virginia. My mother had been a political appointee. That was the extent of my experience—well OK I ran for student government president in college. I was a novice, but I was driven by the belief that if you were not part of the solution you are part of the problem. I also believed that one person can make a difference and the political atmosphere needed to change in Illinois.

Our state was full of corruption on both sides of the aisle. The only way to rid the state of corruption was to replace them with people of moral character. This could be done via prosecution and/or voting people in and out. Both processes would take time and effort but we had to start somewhere. There were others who were likeminded trying to restore integrity to the political process. I would soon meet them and we would partner in an attempt to make a difference.

My journey as a candidate would begin running for Lt Governor. I had been impressed by the candidacy of Michael Steele, Lt. Governor of Maryland and Janette Bradley Lt Governor of Ohio. They had both helped the GOP win the Governor's mansion in their respective states. I thought why not here in Illinois. I had originally thought about running for State Senate because I knew I was a novice and had no idea what lay ahead of me. I felt that running for Lt Governor for my first office was biting off more than I could chew. Until I spoke with a former Lt Governor candidate (Jack) who persuaded me that it was more probable to be elected Lt Governor than to be elected state senator in the heavily democratically populated south suburbs of Chicago. Jack made sense so I announced that I would run for Lt. Governor in August of 2005. I made the circuit of events with the other candidates for Lt Governor and Governor. I got to know Gidwitz, Oberweis, Brady, Rauschenberger, and Birkett. They were all good candidates and I thought I could be a good Lt under their leadership.

But there was a snafu. People began to wonder whether former Governor Edgar would get in the race. The process became paralyzed waiting for a decision from Edgar. In the meantime, the powers that be were making deals behind closed doors preparing Topinka to run if Edgar did not. Other Gubernatorial candidates started picking running mates. The Lt. Gov. candidates were being paired with Gubernatorial candidates. I was also being asked to run for state senate in my district instead of Lt Governor.

Time was not on our side. The Edgar decision would drag on. There were suggestions that I team up with a Gubernatorial candidate but they were holding back as well. Oberweis[3] seemed more interested in Wegman. Brady was waiting to see what Edgar was going to do. Rauschenberger, I believe had joined with Gidwitz[4]. So Wallace had to make a decision to stay in the race with no money and little backing or jump into the senate race with support from the Republican State Senate Campaign Committee (RSSCC).

I had also been approached by others to run for State Senate. Some promised money and other support, which never materialized. Some offers were sincere some were not. I was quickly being introduced to the workings of the political process from the candidate's perspective. The novice would have to learn on the fly. In this environment it was hard to tell who was your friend and who was not, who would deliver on their promise and who would not.

There are countless stories of those who did not deliver. They promised websites, money, to walk a precinct and give more money. The perpetrators were state senators, and committeemen among others. But I will not dwell on the negative, only to say the political waters

[3] Jim Oberweis gave financial support to my campaign after the primary. He also served on the finance committee for Citizens for Eric Wallace and attended a number of my fundraisers. Jim is also the treasurer for the URF.
[4] Ron Gidwitz also served on the finance committee for Citizens for Eric Wallace and contributed funds in support of the campaign.

are filled with sharks and they know whom they are. Now I know who they are and I will never trust them again.

The bright spots of the campaign were finding people who really wanted to support the effort. One such person called me on the phone. She wanted to meet me and talk to me about running for State Senate against State Senator Maggie Crotty. We met at Cracker Barrel for breakfast. What I didn't know was that I was being vetted to see if the United Republican Fund (URF) would support my candidacy. Fran Eaton questioned me on a number of issues and I guess I passed the "smell test" because later I was appearing before the executive director of the URF, Dennis LaComb.

Meanwhile my parents moved from Pompano Beach, Florida to Flossmoor, Illinois to help with the campaign. Family, friends and church members began to join the Citizens for Eric Wallace.

Somewhere during this process I declared my intention to run for State Senate in the 19th District. The RSSCC promised to pay for my walk cards and $25,000 in support for my run, part of which would go toward a mailing. Although this was more money than I had personally to spend, it was not enough to unseat an incumbent State Senator. They lived up to their promises, except the mailing. I went to their fundraising events, traveled to Washington DC and met with GOP Chairman Ken Mehlman, US Senator McCain and US Rep. Denny Hastert. I got to know State Senate Minority leader Frank Watson, State Senator Christine Radogno, State Senator Steve Rauschenberger and State Senator Dale Righter. The ILGOP should be proud of these State Senators they are all good people and more than competent at their jobs. I admire them all. I would also mention State Senator Dan Rutherford who attended a few fundraisers and State Senator Chris Lauzen who gave me my first check ($1,000) toward my senatorial run. He also came and spoke at one of my fundraisers. These men and woman carry the torch for a fiscally responsible and corruption free government and my hat comes off to them.

Needless to say their support was not enough to make a dent in the heavily Democratic district in which I lived. It would take another organization that would come to my aide and help me become competitive and thus put fear in the heart of my opponent for the first time. The United Republican Fund would pick my race as one they would highlight and support. My race was chosen not because it was one that we could definitely win but because they believed in the candidate. They believed that the message of this candidate espoused had to be heard in a place where Republican ideas are seldom championed. State Senator Rauschenberger[5], president of the URF, informed me that it would take two or three cycles before we could unseat the incumbent. Of course I was not buying what he was selling. I thought he may be right but I had to try to prove him wrong. I had to work as though it were possible to win now rather than later. To the URF this was an investment in the future. For me it was an endorsement of the message and the messenger.

If you have never run for office you don't know how lonely it can be. One of the greatest assets the URF gave to me, besides fundraising, was the help of a college intern named Brian Ferkaluk. He was given to me as a "gift" to help me in my campaign. If it were not for his assistance I would not have knocked on as many doors, or worked the various crowds as hard, or made the impact that we made in the South Suburbs. We knocked on doors that had never been knocked on for a campaign. We had gone where no Republican had gone before. We let people know that there was still a two party system in Illinois and that the Republican Party was not dead, contrary to popular belief. Our presence allowed people to see that the GOP had not forgotten about them but was, instead, asking for their support. While many in the GOP had written the South Suburbs off, including the Cook County leadership, the URF was helping to spread the message that choice in education, lower taxes and economic development were concerns Eric Wallace would champion.

This message started to resonate with the people who heard it. Unfortunately not enough people heard the message because there was not enough money to broadcast it. There was not enough money to broadcast it because few believed we could turn the tide in the South Suburbs. Few believed we could turn the tide because they didn't think people would listen to the message. But their theories were wrong because many did hear the message. A number of people told me they voted for a Republican for the first time in their life. Others said they were independent and were not committed to any party. These were black and white voters. These were the people that the GOP had neglected over the years and it is no wonder they did not vote for Republicans. They had

---

[5]Former Senator Steve Rauschenberger was the largest individual contributor to my campaign. He attended a number of my fundraisers and was a great moral supporter.

never seen one up-close. The URF helped change the perception that the GOP does not care about the black community.

Although I lost by a considerable margin, it was not due to the fact that people didn't agree with the message. It was because people, Democrats and Republicans, were reacting to the War and Bush's (apparent) unwillingness to listen to the electorate. The average person does not distinguish between local or state politics and national politics. They saw Republican and reacted negatively. We had no control over that. Nor did the countless other candidates who lost in that election, especially those who were supposed to win. I still got the typical 23 plus percent for that district which says a lot for a bad year to run as a Republican and for a first time candidate.

The proof that we made an impact came a few months later. I ran for the school board and lost the race by 16 votes. I was leading for the third and final position on the board on election night. But come the following afternoon I was behind by 16 votes. The person who beat me out was a trustee for the Village of Matteson. Now if you are an optimist you see this near victory as progress. If you are a pessimist you see the loss, as another reason Republicans cannot win in the South Suburbs. The amazing thing is that I hardly put up an effort for this post. I attended all the forums but did not knock on one door. I was so exhausted from the State Senate race just a few months prior that I could not get the motivation to walk another street or knock on another door. I met people at the forums and gave out literature there. I did not put up signs until the week of the election. I was spent and trying to recover from the other race. (I had also discovered during the State Senate campaign that I was suffering from type II diabetes.) Losing by 16 votes is a testimony to the work of the State Senate campaign not the school board effort. If I could have raised some money and generated a little more energy I could have been on the school board. With this race we scared the Democrats because they saw this as a steppingstone for another run for State Senate in four years. They were correct. But they were wrong to think this loss would deter me. They don't know me very well.

I am an optimist. I see victory written all over the election results and the board of the URF should see victory as well. They stood up when others were sitting down. They gave help while others looked away. They wrote checks when others wrote us off. There is no truer victory, no truer hero than when the outcome is in doubt. When the odds are overwhelmingly against you the underdog rises to do battle anyway. I say bravo for those who have the courage and fortitude to stand with them (me) and fight the good fight. Because the War is not won in one battle but in the skirmishes we face everyday and the fights we choose to engage in. The URF chose to stand with me and fight in the arena of ideas and plant in the minds of people of the South Suburbs that we will champion their cause if you give us the chance. Their response was you have to earn our trust. We began that process in 2006 and 2007. My thanks go out to United Republican Fund, the RSSCC and the many volunteers who worked so hard for the cause.[6]

One thing I have learned from this experience is that no one can win if you don't think you can. No one can guarantee a victory, but you can guarantee a loss by not having a candidate. People who declare that we can't win ought to sit down and shut up. Pessimism never helped anyone accomplish anything. It sucks the air out of the room and chokes the life out of faith. Give no place to pessimism. Stick a gag in its mouth. Cut off its air supply. Starve it to death and don't try to revive it.

Optimism or faith must rule the day. It is the fuel that lights the fire and keeps the motor running. It tells you, "you can" even when the odds are stacked against you. It believes in spite of unbelief. We went to the moon because we believed we could, not because it was possible at the time. In the New Testament Jesus deals with the disciples self doubt after they failed to cast out a demon. In Matthew 17:20, "He said to them, 'you of limited faith, I tell you truly. If you have the faith like the size of a mustard seed plant, you could speak to this mountain, 'depart from here to there' and it will depart. Nothing would be impossible for you." There is much that can be said about this text but I will focus on the application on believing that nothing is impossible. The idea here is that faith is an enabler. It enables you to accomplish any goal. Yet the opposite is also true. Nothing gets accomplished if you don't believe you can accomplish the task, no matter how small it may be.

The biblical text also speaks of doing what God has called one to do and believing in not only God's ability to do the thing but

[6]Thanks go out to my family. My parents Dr. Joan and John Wallace, my sons Eric and Greg, my brothers Victor and Mark, my cousins Vittorio and Sandra Wallace and Randy Livingston for their support. My friends who worked the campaign with me include Maston Knowles, Samira Robinson, Fran Eaton, Michele Santiago, Carmen Anderson, Stage, Pastor Rick Kennedy, George Pearson, Walter Amos, Bridgett Philips, Darlene Shaw, Michelle Muhammad and Jennifer Salley.

believing that God will use you as His vessel to get the thing done. Faith is not placed in our own innate ability but in the ability of God to use us in His service to accomplish His task. This does not mean that every time we attempt a task that everything will go smoothly or turn out the way we planned it. But it will have a positive outcome. A call to run for office does not mean you will necessarily win. A call to a specific task does not mean the task will be completed the way you think it should. An interesting illustration bears this out.

This story is about a man who was given a task by God. He was told to push on a big boulder that was in his yard. Each day the man would faithfully come out and push and push but it would not move. Months went by with the same result. Soon the man became discouraged that his labor had not moved the boulder one inch. He decided to complain to God.

God asked him what was wrong? The man complained that he had worked for days and months on end and had not moved the boulder one inch. God looked at him with compassion and said, "I never told you to move the boulder, I just told you to push on it. In your obedience to me you have accomplished a lot. Look at the muscles in your legs and arms they have increase in strength. Your body is fit and toned. Your stamina has increased exponentially. I will now move the boulder for you because you are now ready for a new task."

This illustration is about faithful obedience. Sometimes one task is used to get us ready for another and to test our obedience to God's will. God's call to action does not mean the task will be completed the way we think it should be completed. God's actions and plans transcend our ability to comprehend therefore He fills us in on a need to know basis. Our job is to be obedient despite the apparent outcome. He knows the ending before we even begin. We are to trust and obey whether we comprehend or not. Ultimately it is God who moves the obstacles in our path anyway. He uses us as partners in His plan. His plan in this illustration was to prepare the man for other strenuous work.

The run for State Senate and School Board could be preparation for another run down the road. As a result of these two elections many people now know my name. They also know what I stand for. They know that I am ready to fight for what I believe. Only God knows what the future holds because He holds and shapes the future. I am just a servant of the Lord trying to do the best I can to glorify His name in faithful obedience to His directives.

Although I ran as a Republican and support the party my first allegiance is to God. If the GOP were to abandon the principles that I hold dear not even their stellar legacy on civil rights could keep me involved. I am a Republican because of the legacy, but most importantly because of the moral issues and social concerns that dominate the platform. I would suggest to anyone that principle should always trump Party affiliation, Democrat or Republican.

My convictions about my faith and party affiliation led to the establishment of Wallace Multimedia Group, LLC. This business was launched in 2007 but the business plan was written in 2005. Our intent in 2005 was to publish a few Christian magazines. Then it morphed into magazines, books, computer animation and video games all with Christian worldview. Running for office delayed the launch but also changed part of the focus.

Running for office opened my eyes to the need for a black conservative magazine that would challenge the Church community to take a closer look at how they spend their vote. Our propensity for voting without understanding the issues has been detrimental to us as a community. Like the pastors in Nashville, we sometimes support an agenda that does not help our plight, but makes it worse. African Americans attend Church more than any race of people in the US. But we don't always vote our conservative values. We have voted what others have told us was in our best interest. We have not always lined up our vote with biblical principle. Therefore we vote people in office just because they are black. We vote people in just because someone is a Democrat, regardless of where they stand on the issues.

We vote for more taxation without understanding how that affects our own earning and spending power. We are told it only affects the "rich." They never define who the "rich" are. Nor are we told that many of these policies and higher taxes prevent you and me from becoming "rich." So in trying to take money from one segment of society and allowing government to distribute it to another segment of society really helps no one. It just gives those in government more control over your life and assets.

African American's dependence on the federal government has not generated one millionaire. But we are constantly told that we need more government programs to fix our problems.

As the president and CEO of Wallace Multimedia Group. LLC, I felt that the black community needed to hear a voice other than the mainstream media, which although liberal on many issues, continues to portray blacks as poor and uneducated. We are much more than the 25% that are below the poverty level. Do we have problems? Yes. But the solution is not in more government but more participation of the black Church and the staunch adherence to traditional family values.

My run for office and involvement in politics made me aware that the African American community needs to be reminded of her history and be reconnected to the values that made her strong. The failures in our communities are because we have failed to hold people accountable from the politician to the preacher. We had, at times, voted with our eyes closed and followed without asking where we were going. This is unacceptable. The "following the leader" mentality without holding the leader accountable is no longer tolerable.

New Orleans is a prime example of the dysfunction of government and the culpability of the people who continue to elect incompetence. The tragedy of Katrina, regardless of the Federal government's failures, only exposed the poverty that was already present in what was once the murder capital of America. The poverty of New Orleans cannot be blamed on the Federal government, as many disingenuous people would have you believe. The poverty of New Orleans rests at the feet of the people of New Orleans, the State of Louisiana and the people they elect to office. The people have to want to escape poverty first. Then they have to elect people who will help facilitate that move. Contrary to popular belief among many African Americans, the government cannot and should not lift people out of poverty. It should help remove some of the obstacles or barriers and give one a hand up not a hand out. The people of New Orleans showed that they did not understand this principle and voted their Mayor back in office. The citizens of Louisiana will probably make the same mistake and vote the Governor back in office.[7] Neither of these actions holds the government accountable for their blatant mishandling of the catastrophe. It is easier to blame the Whitehouse for something they had no control over. It is easier to blame an unpopular president for the incompetence that should lie at the feet of the Mayor and Governor. This is the blind leading the blind and it needs to stop.

Because of situations like New Orleans and the black communities propensity to not vote its interests, Wallace Multimedia Group, LLC (WMG) decided to publish Freedom's Journal Magazine (www.freedomsjournalmagazine.com). The magazine will challenge the African American community in general and the black Church in particular to vote its values and hold elected officials accountable. The magazine is named after the first black newspaper published in 1827. The editors of that paper said, "We wish to plead our cause. Too long have others spoken for us. Too long has the public been deceived by misrepresentations, in things which concern us dearly." We believe this statement to be true today, but also believe that our cause requires that we stand for what we say we believe, and that we actively engage in the political process that represents us.

[7] After the writing of this book the people of Louisiana elected a new Governor, Bobby Jindal. He is the first non-white Governor since P.B.S. Pinchback, the first black Governor of any US state. Both Pinchback and Jindal hail from the Republican Party. Kathleen Blanco, the Democrat governor during Katrina, did not run for re-election.

My challenge to the Church is to stand for what we say we believe, to explore the positions of both parties. Then supporting the candidate that supports the principled agenda that helps transform our neighborhoods and paves the way to producing wealth and health for our children and children's children, because the status quo will not do. Giving our votes away without accountability is political suicide, which leads to impoverishment not empowerment. To be empowered means we allow both parties to court our votes. We hold both parties accountable. We run as candidates in both parties. We celebrate victory when our values are upheld in either party, when our schools begin to educate again, neighborhood streets are walkable, and opportunity, regardless of race, is abounding. Then we will understand that all things are possible for him who believes. This is our goal with FJM. This is my goal as a candidate for office and a minister of the gospel.

The following quote captures the sentiment that I believe the African American community needs to embrace in order to change the cycle of destructive behavior and thought. The italicized words are mine.

> I do not choose to be a common man. It is my right to be uncommon—if I can. I seek opportunity to develop whatever talents God gave me—not security. *I will not cultivate negative stereotypes nor judge others because of their hue; neither will I seek privilege or advantage based on complexion.* I do not wish to be a kept citizen, humbled and dulled by having the state look after me. I want to take the calculated risk; to dream and to build, to fail and to succeed. I refuse to barter incentive for a dole. I prefer the challenges of life to the guaranteed existence; the thrill of fulfillment to the stale calm of utopia. I will not trade freedom for beneficence

nor my dignity for a handout. I will never cower before any master nor bend to any threat. It is my heritage to stand erect, proud and unafraid; to think and act for myself, enjoy the benefit of my creations, and to face the world boldly and say, with *God's help*, this I have done. All this is what it means to be an *African* American.

—Eric Wallace adapted from Dean Alfange

CHAPTER 6

Political Issues

M any of the following articles were written during my run for State Senate in Illinois. Some of these articles address local issues, some address national issues. Those without dates were written for a blog in 2007.

Education

July 27, 2006   *The key to improving education is empowering parents*

I am sure there are some drawbacks to parental choice in education, but we have to consider it as a viable option to the defective educational system now in place. Neither more money nor playing musical chairs with teachers will solve the problem of the current educational system. Only a radical shift of power from the school board and teacher's unions to the parents will solve this problem. The key to improving education is empowering parents.

In recent months there has been a lot of talk about improving education. A certain state senator and the Governor went through a well-choreographed song and dance routine about school funding. Now the same state senator has chosen a new dance partner named Daley, and is calling for more qualified teachers in urban schools. I say to the state senator, the governor, Mayor Daley and anyone else considering joining this bandwagon, school reform will never happen until we empower parents to choose the school their child attends.

Imagine this - a parent with the option to send his/her child to any school they choose, with the money to pay for it. For argument's sake let's make the amount $5,000.00. So a single parent in a low-income district now has the power of a consumer who has $5000.00 to spend (per child). How do you think this parent will be treated by school administration? How will the teachers, knowing that the parent has the power to infuse the school with $5000.00 or take it away, treat this parent and child? It would be like walking into a car dealership with money hanging out your pockets. The parent, like the car buyer would be able to choose the make, model, color and all the bells and whistles the car (dealership) had to offer.

This scenario redistributes the power. It takes it from the administrators and the teachers unions and gives it to the parents where it belongs. Parents become the consumers with a choice as to where they send their kids. The schools become the providers of the product, that is, education, and must deliver that product on time and in a satisfactory manner or they lose their customers. If their product is woefully inferior they will eventually shut down like any poorly run business. And like any business venture a new one will rise up to take its place to provide the needed service for that community.

The end result will be better schools, better teachers, better administrators, better-educated students, and fewer drop-outs. Surely the governor, Mayor and state senators would all agree that parental choice, which empowers the parent, makes the schools accountable and improves our child's education, is the right choice to make. Understanding this is key to improving our educational system.

April 10, 2006   *School funding: When you do the math the answers don't add up*

Parents should be livid to find out that the hard-earned money allotted for their child's school might not make any difference in the quality of that child's education. Many take that old adage that if you give the schools more money they will perform better for gospel truth. Is it our busy schedules or our trust in the system that keep us from closely tracking the details of the funding and implementation of school programs?

It didn't take much time or curiosity for me to find out some startling information about how the funds given and education received might not mean a thing. A little investigation on the web led me to discover that schools within the same district spending the same amount of money had very different educational outcomes. Case in point:

Bremen Community High School District 228 has three high schools. All receive the same amount of money $7,283 per student for instructional expenditure and $12,031 per student for operational expenditures according to the Interactive Illinois Report Card (http://iirc.niu.edu/default.html). Oak Forest H. S. in 2004 had 56% of its students meeting or exceeding the state standard. In 2005 they had 65% meeting or exceeding the state standard. Hillcrest H. S. in 2004 had 33% of its students meeting or exceeding the state standard. In 2005 it had gone down to 31%. They are now on academic watch status (AWS). Tinley Park H. S. in 2004 had 55% of its students meeting or exceeding the state standards. In 2005 they had 51% of its students meeting or exceeding the state standards. How is it that Oak Forest is getting better results with the same amount of money? If we give Hillcrest more money will they do better?

More money does not solve the problem. Thornton TWP H.S. district 205 spent about $8,569 on instructional and $12,621 for operational costs. All three of their High Schools are on academic watch status. In 2005 less than 35% of the students in district 205's High Schools met or exceeded the state standards. One of the worst was Thornton Township H. S. which had only 16% of its students meeting or exceeding the state standards. It's very clear that the numbers just don't add up, and this should give parents reason for pause, especially when they find out that Lincoln Way Central HS in Frankfort spends just over $4500.00 per student in instructional cost and $8,000 in operational costs and 72% of their students, as of 2005, met or exceeded the state standard.

They spent approximately $4,000 less per student than District 205 and $3,000 less than District 228.

The same is true in school after school. The more money a district spends does not mean a better quality education. The problem is that there are several questions that need to be addressed - How should we fund our schools? How do we increase the quality? And how do we spend the money we have?

If we want to improve our schools we must stop listening to those who want to throw good money into bad programs. We must begin to ask the right questions before we will ever get the right answers. This is a test for the parents and teachers. Except in this test you have to come up with the right questions before you get the right answers. We cannot afford to get this wrong or fail this exam. The education of our children is at stake. The old stalwart answer is "let's spend more money." It sounds good but does not address the problem. What we need to do is examine those schools that seem to have gotten it right and try to duplicate their success. Let us spend our money wisely so that it brings good and measurable results, and not throw our money at the problem hoping that it just goes away. As it stands, the only thing that's going away is our money, not the problem. Neither parents nor kids can afford this.

Healthcare
June 28, 2006 Short sighted goals in healthcare have long range consequences

In recent months there has been talk about how the hospitals are not giving back to the communities they serve. Lisa Madigan has gone as far as to propose a bill that would force hospitals to perform more "charity care." Her proposal was to set a standard for the number of patients (or percentage) the hospitals had to see for little or no payment. The proposal was set at the same rate as their tax exemption (about 8%).

There are two problems with this proposal. First, making hospitals do charity care is another form of taxation. It ultimately wipes out any benefit the hospital had with a tax-exempt status. Second, this proposal does not take into account the other service that the hospitals perform in their communities. In the South Suburbs, where industry is basically nonexistent, hospitals are one of the largest employers. If you increase the financial burden on the local hospital the end result will be layoffs and cutbacks. If a hospital cannot meet its financial obligations they will eventually close down. In this scenario no one wins.

Instead of attacking hospitals we should try to come up with solutions that are a win—win for hospitals and the communities they serve. Hospitals are already over burdened with Medicaid patients using the emergency room for non-emergencies. Thanks to Rod Blagojevich we have more people on Medicaid than ever before overtaxing the system even more. Many of these patients use hospitals as their primary care. To alleviate this problem we should encourage the building and utilizing of health clinics such as Ingalls urgent care facility in Flossmoor and Friend Family Health Centers in Chicago. These facilities are designed to handle Medicaid patients, patients without insurance. They would help alleviate the influx of patients into the emergency rooms who do not have a real emergency. The clinics would become the primary care facility for those without a primary physician.

The last piece to solving this problem is for the state to pay its bills on time. Medicaid payments are about two months in the arrears. The Democrat's solution is to tax the hospitals or make them do more charity care. How short sighted is that? So tell me, who will care for these people or provide jobs once the hospitals close down? It is this kind of thinking that threatens the stability and prosperity of our great State. It is short-sighted politicians who only care about reelection and not true public service who implement these short-sighted strategies. We need to devise long-range plans for long-term solutions before our hospitals and the communities they serve, become charity cases.

Economics and Taxes

March 7, 2007 *The Cost of Living (Wages) and Taxes*

I had a conversation with a friend of mine several months ago. She (let's call her Betty) had expressed her concern about the cost of food at McDonald's. Betty could not understand why her salad and filet-o-fish cost as much as they did. We both remembered a time when you could by a hamburger, fries, and a shake for under a buck.

I then explained to her that the cost of doing business continues to rise. Therefore the cost to the consumer rises also. I gave the example of the effect an increase in labor costs has on the economy. If you increase the cost of labor (or taxes), especially artificially through mandated increases, these increases will be passed onto the consumer. The more it costs to produce a Big Mac the more it will cost you to purchase it.

Betty asked why the business could not absorb the increasing costs and keep their prices low. I told her that entrepreneurs were not in business to break even or perform a charitable community service. They bring to the market place a product or service that they believe the general public needs. In exchange for that product or service they expect to earn a living through the profits they make.

Betty is a proponent of a living wage and higher taxes on the business community, but has no idea what that really means to our economy or to her purchasing power. Some times good-meaning people support good meaning ideas that have devastating consequences. As the old proverb states, "the road to hell is paved with many good intentions."

In a noble desire to lift people out of poverty a "living wage" would just exacerbate the problem and give people a false sense of accomplishment. Raising the minimum wage or creating a "living wage" is an exercise in futility. First of all you must answer the question how much should a "living wage" be? Is it $10, $20 or $30 dollars an hour? How will you account for the increase in prices that this mandate will induce? As the cost of production goes up so does the price to the consumer. There is no way around this principle.

If you pay a person $20 an hour to flip burgers, which is about three times what it is now, it will be reflected in the cost to purchase the burger. Therefore any gain that these well-intended people had of lifting someone out of poverty is never realized because the prices do not stay the same. The cost of goods and services will increase in proportion to the labor cost or tax increases. In this scenario poor people do not gain any ground. They are still poor and at the bottom of the earning scale.

Unless you want to follow in the footsteps of Hugo Chavez and let the government dictate the cost of labor, goods and services than you must let the free market be the determining factor.

The only remedy to help poor people become middle class and others to improve their earning power is to do what rich people do. Use the system to their advantage. The old proverb says that, "it is better to light a candle than curse the darkness." We light a candle when we take the measures necessary that will improve our ability to command a higher salary such as: job training, returning to school, starting a business, or a combination of these.

Government should only get involved where it helps to level the playing field or create incentives. For instance government should not start job-training programs but create incentives for businesses to do so. A good job-training program will help develop a person's set of skills. With increased skills comes increased demand, which leads to an increase in salary and upward mobility. The salary increase means that person pays more taxes, helping the government retrieve the tax break that was given to the corporation to train the unskilled worker.

This is a win-win scenario. The corporation gets a better skilled worker. The worker gets a skill that commands more pay. The government gets its tax incentive back. All this happens without upsetting the free market and raising false expectations.

Betty did not understand this until it was explained to her. Unfortunately, there are a number of Betties out there. Many of them are running for office as aldermen, US Senators and Presidential hopefuls.

Their good intentions are misguided and sometimes disingenuous as they pander to the Betties in the general public.

If they have their way a hamburger, fries and a shake will cost what we are now charged to eat steak, potatoes and drink a glass of wine. How does this help the poor?

We need real solutions for real problems, to help real people. What we don't need is the illusion of parity that results as a consequence of hype.

April 3, 2007 What would Milton say about IL's ComEd dilemma?

I am perplexed at the number of Republicans who say freezing electric rates is a good idea. I wonder what brilliant economist Milton Friedman would say if he were alive today? No I don't, there's no question: Milton would be disappointed that the free market ideas he espoused had somehow been lost in finding the best solution.

ComEd is not to blame for the situation in which we find ourselves. It's the fault of the Illinois General Assembly. Ten years ago, they froze electric rates while looking at ways to promote a competitive free market for utilities. Someone understood that a free market, with companies competing for customers would not only reduce prices, but also improve service. Sounds good, right? Milton would have agreed.

But the legislature failed to do its job. Ten years passed without a plan or proposal to create a free utilities market. Now they want the utilities to pay for the legislature's lack of due diligence. I think not. Freezing prices, again, goes against every free market principle Republicans claim they believe in.

So what would Milton have us do?

How about taking the raise that the legislature gave itself and using those funds to assist customers in a one-time rebate to set off the increase in their electric bills? This is a win-win proposal. People will be helped to pay the increase. Utilities will gather in a few bucks and the legislature will be provided with a much-needed incentive to focus on the long term problem.

As long as a utility monopoly exists, rates will be high and service sub par. Competition encourages fair pricing and better service. Monopolies don't have to improve because the consumer has no other options. There is no choice for service.

This same principle, frankly, applies to the public school monopoly and the one party political system in Chicago. But these are subjects for another day.

Let's be creative and find innovative ways to fix this problem, instead of passing the buck.

There's no question, Milton would agree.

Republicans vs Democrats

October 1, 2005   *The New Slave Master (part I)*

The trauma that Katrina brought to our shores has uncovered what some are calling the "racial divide." The divide between races that becomes evident when one looks at the same event and comes to a totally different conclusion. An article appeared in USA Today Sept.13, 2005, entitled, "Poll shows racial divide on storm response," tries to illuminate this point. The article suggested that blacks and whites saw the slow response to the victims of Katrina through different colored spectacles. Whites wanted to blame the residences and the local government while blacks laid the blame on the federal government. It is true that these are generalities, but they are representative of the overall populace.

The article in USA Today comes up short in that it never explores the reason(s) for the divide, but I will attempt to pose a theory. The problem is in our own understanding of what we think government is supposed to do. The poor, including blacks, have long believed that the federal government is supposed to take care of them. This understanding of the federal government is in error. I believe that the government helps provide a level playing field, but ultimately we are responsible for playing the game. For instance, when the emancipated slaves ventured out into the workforce to support themselves many became lawyers, doctors, preachers, and even politicians. The federal government passed the 14th and 15th amendment giving blacks full citizenship and voting rights. Because of this leveling of the playing field many blacks took advantage of this new opportunity and ran for office. Five years after emancipation the first blacks were in congress (all republican). They were former slaves with little or no formal education who sought a better life for themselves and their families. They were not relying on the government to hand them prosperity—they went after it on their own. Frederick Douglas, when speaking about the future of former slaves said:

> Our destiny is largely in our own hands. If we find, we shall have to seek. If we succeed in the race of life it must be by our own energies, and by our own exertions. Others may clear the road, but we must go forward, or be left behind in the race of life.

Those who did not flee New Orleans in the face of Katrina are a symbol of people who have been left behind, both literally and figuratively. They placed their trust in the government to take care of them, but it could not. Thus, when the City and State government failed many blamed the federal government for not overriding the local government. This mindset is part of that slave mentality that believes someone else is responsible for our plight. As the old slave master once told us where to live, when to eat, when to talk, when to work, where to sleep, what to eat, so now does government. The City government told people to leave but did not provide transportation. The dependence on the new master was misplaced, as is any undue reliance on anything or anyone other than God. Neither the federal government nor the local government is responsible for one's lot in life or one's initiative or lack thereof. As Ben Franklin once said, "the constitution provides us the right to pursue happiness, but we must catch it for ourselves."

The problem in New Orleans and in much of black America is the thought that the government should take care of us. The government has become the new master. Many government programs that make people more dependent and less independent have fostered this attitude. Our dependence on a bureaucratic government drains one of initiative and creativity. It sucks the life out of hope for a better future. It retards and hinders the persistence that drives us to fulfill our dreams. Government, the federal government in particular, does not make dreams come true-- it can only make them possible. The onus is on us to make it happen. Again Frederick Douglas says:

> If we remain poor and dependent, the riches of other men will not avail us. If we are ignorant, the intelligence of other men will do but little for us. If we are foolish, the wisdom of other men will not guide us. If we are wasteful of time and money, the economy of other men will only make our destitution the more disgraceful and hurtful.

Dependence on government at any level will leave one poor and destitute. Welfare, Medicaid, food stamps, and other programs were meant to be a safety net not a way of life. Unfortunately many people, black and white, have viewed government programs as an end instead of a means to an end.

Republicans have always touted that while Democrats offer a "handout," Republicans offer a "hand-up." This is not to say that at times, especially times of disaster, we may need a handout-- but to remain in the handout line is to perpetuate dependency. To become independent one must transition from the handout line into the hand-up line. For too long we have been in the handout line waiting for the new master to give us what he deems is best for us. The results are the large numbers of poor blacks in the inner cities (which are normally controlled by democrats—

the handout people!) Instead we should be clamoring to get into the hand-up line and become more self-sufficient, fulfilling our hopes and dreams.

August 4, 2005   *Lynching: Who should apologize?*

The recent US Senate's apology for its failure to enact anti-lynching legislation this summer has given some an occasion to point the finger of racism. They point to the fact that a number of Republicans did not sign the apology. Therefore, they assume that these Republicans, as most Republicans, must be racist. Forgive me for asking a simplistic question, but isn't an apology supposed to come from those who perpetrated the crime? If you have not committed an act of offense, why apologize? An apology in and of itself assumes you have done something wrong of which you need absolution.

As I look at history, it was the Democrat Party that instituted lynching. It was originally propagated to keep blacks from voting republican after the federal troops left the South. Following the emancipation of the slaves in 1865, blacks were given the right to vote by the 15th amendment in February 1870. This was problematic for many southern states since blacks sometimes out numbered whites 3 to1. Consequently, blacks who ran as Republicans were elected overwhelmingly to state wide office at that time.

The Democrats could not tolerate being governed by their former slaves. Thus, they concocted a number of schemes to limit black's access to the polls. The most infamous group used to carry out the Democrat's plot was the Klu Klux Klan. One of the most gruesome tools in their arsenal was lynching. They did not limit their attacks on blacks, but also attacked white Republicans who dedicated themselves to seeing black people free to enjoy the liberties afforded them in the 15th Amendment. Of the 4,743 people lynched, between 1882 and 1964, 3,446 were black and 1,297 were white.

The House passed a number of anti-lynching laws between 1920 and 1940, while the Democrat controlled Senate passed none. The Senate defeated every bill that came from the House design to abolish lynching.

So who should apologize? Should the Republicans apologize for fighting slavery, discrimination and lynching? Or should the Democrats for not only failing to stop lynching but promoting it via its perpetrators, the KKK? Given these facts, you decide.

Party Reform

March 28, 2007 *Honor, Loyalty and Singleness of Purpose*

A few days ago I took my sons, now young men, to see the movie "300." When you get past the blood and guts, the over the top portrayals of the Persians as weird freaky people, you begin to see a theme. Their single purpose and dedication was to protect their way of life, their families and comrades in arms. They had trained their whole life for war.

But this is not what is impressive. What impressed me was that when they fought they fought as one. Their battle formations were quite imposing. Each man was to use his shield to protect the man to his side from shoulder to thigh. They moved insync, shoulder to shoulder, as one unit. What bonded them were honor, loyalty, and singleness of purpose, dare I say we lack these virtues today.

Where is the honor in our society today? What does it even mean to be honorable? Where is the honor in our party? In the movie to be honorable was to do what was right regardless of the consequences. To be loyal was to stand with your countrymen, your friends, and in one case a son standing with his father. Their singleness of purpose was to protect their homeland from the coming invader who would make them slaves. They fought to keep their land and their people free from the tyranny of the Persian Empire.

In the movie the small band of 300 men withstood countless attacks of the Persian armies until being surrounded by overwhelming numbers. Even then they refused to surrender in the end attempting one last assault at trying to kill the emperor Xerxes.

In an attempt to discourage the other Greek City States from fighting, Xerxes sends the King Leonidas' body parts across Greece. It had the opposite effect. The City States that had been warring against each other joined together to repel the Persian army. The story of the brave 300 inspired the fragmented nation to victory. What bonded the Greeks were honor, loyalty and singleness of purpose.

They honored the bravery and sacrifice of the 300 men. Their loyalty was to Greece, their countrymen, villages and families whom they vowed to protect. Their singleness of purpose was to defeat the enemy at their doorsteps. Thus, the Persians never defeated Greece.

I wonder what has happened to our sense of honor, loyalty and singleness of purpose? I am not advocating that we adapt the Spartan society. Much of what Spartan society entailed would not be welcomed today. But virtues of selflessness are never antiquated or passé. They are enduring and endearing virtues of character that have somehow been lost in our quest for individual glory, and self-aggrandizement.

One could argue that loyalty and singleness of purpose are still around. But they are loyalty to ones own family with the purpose of protecting ones power and position. We see evidence of this in state and local politics every day. What we are missing is honor which guides loyalty and singleness of purpose. Without honor we become selfish and not selfless. I believe a lack of honor is the reason many have lost faith in the political process, our school system, and even our churches. We sacrifice principle for expediency. We make deals with the devil for a fleeting moment of glory. We sell our souls for a bowl of soup. Then wonder why our kids are on drugs, our taxes are high, and criminal activity pervades every level of state and local government.

I pray to God that we regain a sense of honor, loyalty and singleness of purpose portrayed in the movies (Brave Heart, Remember the Titans, Amazing Grace, 300, Pride, and others). I would hate to think that honor is only found on a movie screen. But that a few brave men and women who stand against corruption and evil will arouse in us the slumbering spirit. As Greece was aroused to action by the honorable sacrifice of 300 men may we be aroused to action by those who place themselves under public scrutiny and honorably run for office. May they run with loyalty to their constituents, and party, but foremost with principle, with singleness of purpose to make their towns, counties and state a better place for all to live, work and play. Remembering that "evil is powerless if the GOOD are unafraid" (Ronald Reagan).

March 8, 2007 *The Party of Freedom*

As I watched the movie Amazing Grace, I was struck by the fact that William Wilberforce and the other abolitionist never gave up in their battle to free human beings from slavery. Their persistence won the day in the decapitating of the slave trade. It also occurred to me that the Republican Party was founded with that same spirit, which led to the freedom of American slaves. I have tried to rekindle the memory of such a spirit, to remind the party of its great accomplishments. I feel compelled to do so again.

It is not about black or white, rich or poor, or even theological persuasion. It is about freedom! The Republican Party has always stood for Freedom.

We believe in freedom from overtaxation. Government at any level should learn how to govern with fiscal restraint. The federal government especially needs to treat each and everyone fairly, not taxing or over burdening person, class or business. We believe that the people know better how to spend their hard earned money than the government. Thus we propose a "Fair Tax" system.

We believe in the freedom of the market place of ideas. It is in this market place that wealth is created. The wealth of knowledge, wealth of ideas, wealth of commerce, wealth of ingenuity, a wealth that is unparalleled in human history. The market place is the engine for progress. Over regulation is the acid that corrodes the wheels. The free market rewards hard work, so when preparation meets with opportunity, success is assured.

We believe in the freedom to choose what schools our children attend. We call this parental or school choice. We share the idea that one school system, that reflects, "One size fits all," cannot adequately teach a diversity of kids with various learning styles. We believe that a good education is a real entitlement that only comes through a diversity of options, not conformity to a mediocre standard. Choice will allow every kid, regardless of race, religion or social status, who has a desire to learn, a chance to find success and prosperity, a chance to fulfill their destiny.

We believe in the freedom that good health affords. Yet we believe that freedom should be exercised with the ability to choose our health care providers. We believe health care should be affordable, portable and manageable. It will be affordable when health providers must compete. It becomes portable as we allow individuals to own their health care plan. It is manageable when the state is not responsible for paying the entire bill.

We believe in the freedom to improve one's condition in life. Many have migrated to our shores from overseas and across our land borders. We welcome them with open arms but believe that this should be done in accordance with our judicial system. We are a nation where the rule of law means something. These laws are established to keep order and hold chaos at bay. These laws where established by legislators who were elected "of the people, by the people, for the people."

We believe in the freedom to choose life. We take great pains to protect life against those who would throw it away like they discarded trash. Thus we protect with great vigor the life of the unborn, the elderly and the oppressed. We dispatch legislation, food and troops to protect those who cannot protect themselves. We stand in harms way to turn back starvation, genocide and subjugation. For we understand that "no one is free until we all are free."

Ladies and gentlemen we stand for these and other freedoms, for which many have died to protect. Many have spent themselves and their fortunes to ensure that everyone would have an opportunity to "life, liberty and the pursuit of happiness." I say bravo to William Wilberforce, Charles Sumner, and Thaddeus Stevens. They paved the road for Lincoln, Grant and Dirksen.

Yet, somehow I think it is time for an encore.